Lost Generation

Lost Generation

The Story Of Cambodian Rock & Roll

Susan Fletcher Haythorpe

Copyright © 2021 Susan Fletcher Haythorpe

The moral right of the author has been asserted.

Apart from any fair dealing for the purposes of research or private study, or criticism or review, as permitted under the Copyright, Designs and Patents Act 1988, this publication may only be reproduced, stored or transmitted, in any form or by any means, with the prior permission in writing of the publishers, or in the case of reprographic reproduction in accordance with the terms of licences issued by the Copyright Licensing Agency. Enquiries concerning reproduction outside those terms should be sent to the publishers.

Matador
9 Priory Business Park,
Wistow Road, Kibworth Beauchamp,
Leicestershire. LE8 0RX
Tel: 0116 279 2299
Email: books@troubador.co.uk
Web: www.troubador.co.uk/matador
Twitter: @matadorbooks

ISBN 978 1800461 314

British Library Cataloguing in Publication Data.
A catalogue record for this book is available from the British Library.

Printed and bound by CPI Group (UK) Ltd, Croydon, CR0 4YY
Typeset in 12pt Futura by Troubador Publishing Ltd, Leicester, UK

Matador is an imprint of Troubador Publishing Ltd

For Graham, who brought me to Cambodia in the first place.

Foreword

A few points about the format of this book. Khmer, the Cambodian national language, has its own script for which there's no generally-agreed romanised form; spellings can vary enormously and confusingly so I've opted for the spellings most commonly used. Khmer names appear, as is usual in Cambodia, with family name first unless their individual owners prefer otherwise. As for the titles of the old songs, that depends pretty much upon who you're talking to or where you find them, as the original appellations have frequently been lost along with the vinyl records that bore them.

Contents

Chapter 1	Dance, Dance, Dance	1
Chapter 2	Back to Zero	4
Chapter 3	Golden Years	10
Chapter 4	Ancient and Modern	17
Chapter 5	The First Guitar Heroes	27
Chapter 6	In Their Own Words	38
Chapter 7	Rocking the Boat	53
Chapter 8	Cambodia's Elvis and the Golden Voice	63
Chapter 9	Don't Miss Me	74
Chapter 10	The Collectors	86
Chapter 11	City of Tears	97
Chapter 12	A Journey Through Time and Space	103
Acknowledgements		112
Resources		113

ONE

Dance, Dance, Dance

> *'Let's dance while we are young, the
> band are playing the a-go-go.'*
>
> Pan Ron, *Rom A-go-go*

In the heat of the evening a sultry Phnom Penh shimmies to the sounds that erupt from cafés and dance clubs, from shophouses and transistor radios, *wats* and wedding parties; drinks in the oxygen, feeds on the after-dark adrenaline and exhales a sweet-sour breath of jasmine flowers and *prahok*. The Pearl of Asia, a thriving, cosmopolitan hub where cultures ancient and modern, sacred and profane jostle for standing on the cluttered streets, is wildly, exuberantly alive and swinging.

The city's sonic pulse rides the thick night air along its broad boulevards and snaking, night-cloaked alleys. Over *naga*-tipped pagodas and colonial villas; around the Chaktomuk Theatre's modernist contours; past the red-marbled majesty

Image courtesy CVMA

of the Independence Monument to fashionable nightspots where the capital's movers and shakers, its hipsters and party-makers converge. To the upscale Magasin D'Etat nightclub, where a petite chanteuse with a big voice holds her audience transfixed. Behind her a band pumps out full-bloodied rock and roll; a deliciously dizzying cocktail of searing, psyched-up guitars, soaring keyboards and taut rhythms over which her high, clear, teasing vocals hover. Shaken and stirred, the crowd drinks it in. And they dance. How they dance.

The young woman is Pan Ron and Cambodia adores her. She's talented, vivacious, a famous singer and hugely successful recording artist; in her prime. In just a few, too-short years Pan Ron will be missing, presumed dead. No-one will know for certain how or when she died, only that, like her fellow singers and musicians, artists and intellectuals she was among the masses targeted for systematic execution by the communist dictator Pol Pot's brutal regime. A victim of the hideous genocide that devastated a country and its proud people.

Under the Khmer Rouge and in the name of a pure, classless, agrarian society, the music of Cambodia's Golden Age was lost.

Together with some two million lives and the heart of a nation.

TWO

Back to Zero

'Oh! Phnom Penh, during the three years we were apart, I missed you and my heart ached every day because the enemy separated us.'

Keo Chenda (composer), *Oh! Phnom Penh*

When communist Khmer Rouge forces finally captured Phnom Penh on 17 April 1975, the city's inhabitants had little idea what to expect. Although Cambodia had existed in a state of civil war for the past five years, Pol Pot's army had been operating mainly in the rural provinces, party leaders were covert about their real objectives and little news was allowed to travel about the harrowing developments elsewhere in the country. Curfews may have taken their toll on the city's freedom as the communist forces advanced, food supplies dwindled as the influx of refugees from the provinces grew, and the capital slowly become a shadow of its former, flourishing self, but ordinary life for the Khmer, or ethnic Cambodian people, continued in its own way. And in any case, was their resigned view, what could be worse than living under the current chaotic and repressive Khmer Republic government?

The answer to that question would be far more horrifying than any could have imagined.

Cambodia's Prince Norodom Sihanouk, a shrewd politician and head of state since 1941, had prided himself on remaining neutral in relation to events in Indochina, even with the Vietnam war raging on his country's northern and eastern borders. That carefully-nurtured neutrality and the deeply-entrenched monarchy itself were finally, fatally challenged in 1970 when Sihanouk was deposed, in absentia, by an army led by his prime minister, Lon Nol, and backed by the United States.

The Khmer Rouge had been secretly gathering strength and support and the change of government provided them with a golden opportunity. Taking advantage of the general population's deep-seated support for the monarchy, they allied themselves to the now-exiled Prince. Since 1969 the USA had expanded its aerial bombing of Vietnamese targets to take in rural parts of Eastern Cambodia; the communists found ready supporters in the communities devastated by the shelling.

The fall of Cambodia's capital marked the final stage of the country's takeover by Khmer Rouge troops. What began as a day of hesitant celebration — the soldiers were initially seen as a liberating force, there to free citizens from the unpopular Republican government — became one of confusion, fear and horror.

As Phnom Penh fell to Pol Pot's black pyjama-clad soldiers, the city's residents were forced from their homes at gunpoint on the pretext the city was about to be shelled by US forces. Those who refused to go were shot and the rest marched away to the countryside. Few understood what was happening to them and the journey, much of it on foot and in blistering heat, was brutal in every way. Many of those who had set out on the enforced evacuation accompanied by their families arrived as widows and orphans or else separated from their loved ones and unaware if they were alive or dead. A fresh hell awaited them once they reached their destination: vast, rural labour camps where the Khmer Rouge's extreme experiment in social restructuring was underway.

Khmer Rouge ideology was based on Maoist principles. All commerce would be abolished, as would education, religion, money, private ownership and the rights of the individual. Food and rudimentary medical care would be provided by the state. Pol Pot believed he could take China's Great Leap Forward a stride further. Khmer Rouge victory, he announced, was a triumph over American imperialism; a pure, indeed superior, communist revolution achieved without any outside aid or support. Foreigners were expelled, embassies closed, all media abolished.

Phnom Penh citizens join the enforced exodus of the capital

Cambodia's communist regime would operate in self-imposed isolation from the rest of the world.

The regime set about its 'cleansing' process immediately. The wealthy, the educated, artists and professionals were taken away to 'study'. In fact they were summarily executed. As it became horribly apparent what was at stake, members of the middle classes went to any lengths to hide their background and to save themselves and their families. Among them were the singers and musicians of Cambodia's Golden Age.

Brother Number One

Pol Pot was the *nom de guerre* of Sar Saloth, also known as Brother Number One, a former electronics student from a relatively affluent farming family in Cambodia's Kampong Thom province. The youngest of seven siblings and a serious, hardworking child, nothing in his early life suggested the brutal extremist Sar would become.

Sar was educated in Phnom Penh but failed to excel in his academic career. In 1949, aged 24, he won a scholarship to study electronics at a technical college in Paris where he fell in with a crowd that would change the course of his ambitions and, in the most horrific way, the history of his country.

Sar joined a Marxist circle that included fellow Cambodians who were studying at Parisian universities — students like Khieu Samphan and Leng Sary who would also become main players in the Khmer Rouge — and it was in this keenly politicised, intellectual company that his leftist ideals were honed.

Face of evil: Sar Saloth a.k.a. Pot Pot

He returned to Asia in 1953 having failed key college examinations but primed to join the communist fight against French colonialism. Within a year, however, that fight was over. Norodom Sihanouk had pulled the rug from under the Cambodian communists by shrewdly negotiating his country's independence from France himself.

Cambodia's early communist movement had been largely made up of fragmented groups aligned with the *Vietminh*, the insurgent supporters of Ho Chi Minh across the country's border with Vietnam. Sar was instrumental in the formation of Cambodia's own communist party and in 1962 became its leader. The party's revolutionary zeal was now directed at the monarchy.

Khmer Rouge, or Red Khmer, was the label bestowed upon the communists by Norodom Sihanouk. His suppression of left wing activists in Phnom Penh led the party to take their operations undercover, setting up a clandestine base in the rural highlands by the Vietnamese border. Here they lay low, recruiting members of the local hill tribes to their cause and formulating the policies that would lead to one of history's most appalling genocides.

THREE

Golden Years

> *'Heaven protects our King and gives him
> happiness and glory to reign over
> our souls and our destinies.'*
>
> Nokor Reach, Cambodian National Anthem

In 1955, two years after brokering Cambodia's independence from France, King Norodom Sihanouk, the last of the country's 'god-kings', quit the throne he had occupied for the past 14 years to become its first democratic Head of State. The country's longstanding colonial 'protectors' ejected and the powers of the new king, Sihanouk's father, Norodom Suramarit, reduced to those of a constitutional monarch, the new democracy — the *Sangkum Reastr Niyum*, meaning People's Socialist Community — was his to remodel in his own image: cultured, artistic and abreast of modern European society.

Norodom Sihanouk was a prolific composer

The following 15 years would come to be recognised as Cambodia's Golden Age.

French-educated Sihanouk adored the arts and was not merely a huge supporter and patron of creative endeavour but an enthusiastic practitioner in his own right. He wrote, produced and directed as many as fifty films, a good number of them commercially successful, and was not averse to casting himself in a leading role. A prolific composer, songwriter, poet and an accomplished musician, he even dabbled in interior design and is credited with work on one of Phnom Penh's foremost hotels, the Cambodiana on the city's riverfront.

At a showing of his film *Twilight*, in the South of France in 1970, Sihanouk reportedly addressed the audience to say, 'My family and the entire Khmer people love the arts and practice them willingly. This explains why I can have, unlike other Heads of State, artistic and political activities at the same time.'

The charismatic former king, a politically astute and not uncontroversial figure, saw himself as a benevolent father to his people. Committed to modernisation, he set about an ambitious round of public works and improvements to the country's health and education systems.

As for Phnom Penh, Sihanouk was determined to create for the Khmer nation a capital that would sit proudly alongside the finest in the world. His vision was of a refined garden city of parks and waterways; elegant and harmonious. The city's built profile was overwhelmingly of the French colonial style; a fresh approach was needed to distance Cambodia from its past and create a truly modern identity that would be uniquely its own. The Modernist-inspired movement known as New Khmer Architecture embodied exactly the progressive image that *Sangkum*-era Cambodia aspired to. Under its chief exponent, the architect Vann Molyvann, the movement fused form and function to create a singular architectural style that favoured brutalist construction techniques and borrowed practical and stylistic elements from traditional Khmer dwellings and temples. The public and private buildings that took shape during Cambodia's Golden Age helped to earn Phnom Penh its status as Asia's Pearl.

In the meantime, with Sihanouk's high-profile patronage, the country's film industry was flourishing. Production companies

Phnom Penh's National Sports Complex (Olympic Stadium), designed by architect Vann Molyvann

were established, new cinemas opened and Cambodians flocked to watch homegrown movies instead of foreign imports. The latest features would be proclaimed loudly, through megaphones, from billboard-adorned trucks that toured the capital's streets. Three hundred or so films were made during the *Sangkum*, some of which — like director Tea Lim Kuon's *The Snake King's Wife*, a horror film deserving of cult status not least for requiring one of its young actors to wear a cap made of live snakes — were shown worldwide. Few, however, like the actors and directors behind them, survived the Khmer Rouge. Sihanouk also instigated a series of film festivals and no doubt few were surprised when his own film, *The Little Prince*, won first prize at the inaugural event and another, *Twilight*, scooped the same accolade at the second.

The Art Deco Lux cinema was one of Phnom Penh's most popular picture houses

Above: Surviving movie ticket

Right: Film poster for *The Snake King's Wife*

To further the *Sangkum*'s ambitions for the nation's youth, the Prince established the Royal University of Fine Arts with five departments: Architecture and Urban Planning; Music; Visual Arts; Archeology; and Drama and Choreography. Education here would be Khmer-led unlike that provided by the existing, French-established schools.

Norodom Sihanouk may no longer have occupied the throne but the spirit of cultural liberalism and civic and national pride that he instilled reigned supreme. Phnom Penh became a popular playground for an affluent, arty crowd and a favourite destination for tourists and visitors from around South East Asia and farther afield. It was within this lively, creative milieu that Khmer rock and pop music took shape.

In the late 1950s, the Chinese Prime Minister gave Sihanouk a gift: a 20-kilowatt radio transmitter. Cambodia's aural soundtrack was about to change. By April 1959 the country's first, national radio station, Royal Cambodian Radio, had arrived on-air and soon became a breeding ground for a new generation of singing stars, musicians and songwriters.

The station provided a facility for both broadcasting and recording music. Its early output was conservative in flavour, traditional music and folk ballads, but as more and more musicians began to pick up and experiment with guitars, it opened its doors to the rock and roll scene taking shape in the capital's bars and clubs. Programmes were transmitted through loudspeakers outside the radio station's Phnom Penh HQ, where locals, many of whom could not afford their own radio player, would gather to listen.

The arrival of cheap, widely-available transistor radios in the early 1960s meant that even people living in remote rural areas were able to tune in — and not just to Cambodian broadcasts. As the decade neared its end their transistors were also picking up American Forces Network radio, destined for troops in neighbouring Vietnam. Western rock and pop music had found an eager new audience.

FOUR

Ancient and Modern

*'The forests, the ancient temples that
I love, I will never forget them.'*

HRH King Norodom Sihanouk, *The Enchanted Forest*

That Cambodia's most powerful individual should be such a Renaissance man with a finger in every artistic pie is not so surprising. A look at Cambodia's history reveals a civilisation where cultural pursuits were not just highly valued but an intrinsic part of national identity.

At its height in the 14th century, the Khmer Empire extended beyond the environs of today's Cambodia to encompass Southern Vietnam and the Mekong Delta, Southern Laos and parts of Thailand.

Central to the Empire and the seat of its power and religion — closely linked to the extent that its rulers were held to be semi-divine 'god-kings' — was the vast temple complex of Angkor, a majestic feat of architecture and water engineering. Over the following six decades wars raged, territories were lost to other countries but the ancient, ruined city of Angkor, now protected by UNESCO and one of the world's most visited tourist attractions, remains the chief symbol of Khmer pride.

From the earliest days, music, art and dance have fed the Khmer spirit and informed Cambodian people's approach to life. Numerous images of musicians with instruments much like those played by traditional orchestras today are carved within the ornate bas-reliefs at Angkor Wat along with shapely *apsaras*, celestial dancers whose graceful postures and exquisite hand gestures have become iconic elements of Khmer classical ballet and are still mirrored in the country's popular modern dances.

Apsaras at Angkor Wat

Early Khmer music was mostly religious in nature. The overwhelming majority of Cambodians practise a form of Theravada Buddhism that incorporates a liberal slice of animism, the ancient belief system that predates both Buddhism and Hinduism, which accounts for the prevalence in the country of often ornate shrines to a variety of spirits and ghosts of the dead.

Musicians were held in esteem, their skills revered and passed down through the generations. They played at pagoda ceremonies and other religious and royal functions, performances which, like classical dance, were generally reserved for the elite. The most outstanding musicians and singers were recruited to the King's own troupe — the supergroups of their time — a practice that continued well into the 20th century.

Sadly, few of the great masters of traditional music survived the Khmer Rouge years leaving the music itself under threat. Organisations like Cambodian Living Arts have since stepped in to give the kiss of life to the ancient arts, reviving and preserving time-honoured skills and bringing on a new generation of practitioners.

Mastering the chapei

One of the great living Masters of Cambodian traditional music, the numbers of whom are dwindling rapidly, is Kong Nay, virtuoso of the *chapei dong weng*, a two-stringed instrument resembling a long-necked banjo. His spare musical style and gravelly vocals evoke the sound of the blues, albeit those of the Mekong Delta rather than the Mississippi. With its witty, frequently satirical and generally improvised lyrics, *chapei dong weng* music is thought to have its roots in a tradition of travelling musicians, whose songs would combine popular fables with moral advice. In 2016 it made its way onto UNESCO's official list of Intangible Cultural Heritage in Need of Urgent Safeguarding.

Blind since childhood, Kong Nay says he took up the instrument, which requires considerable skill to master, for want of other ways to make a living. In a 2013 interview for Cambodia Living Arts he described Khmer traditional arts as 'the soul of our country.'

'I can't imagine,' he said, 'what would happen if we lost all these art forms. Without arts a country just looks like a flower growing on rocks, without any beauty. Artists are like birds flying in all directions to spread the culture.'

Master of the chapei Kong Ny

The traditional music most frequently heard in the modern day Kingdom of Cambodia is known as *pin peat*, an arrhythmic, hypnotic mingling of percussion and wind instruments comparable to Thailand's *piphat*, *sep niyai* from Laos and Javanese *gamelan*. *Pin peat* can be heard regularly in *wats* (Cambodian Buddhist temples). Played at ceremonial events, it also accompanies performances of classical dance and the shadow theatre known as *sbek thom* — literally, 'big leather' — another traditional Khmer art form, which uses huge, ornately etched and filigreed buffalo skin images to tell epic religious stories.

A *pin peat* orchestra will typically number eight or nine musicians playing instruments that include the *roneat*, a bamboo xylophone; assorted gongs *(cong)* and drums *(skor)*; and a Khmer oboe called the *srolai*.

The soundtrack to more secular entertainment and gatherings is *mahori* music, similar to the Thai music of the same name, which also dates back to the early Angkorian period. Led by the *tro*, a two stringed instrument (though the *tro Khmer* has three) played with a bow and akin to the fiddle, and a wooden flute called the *khloy*, *mahori* songs are carefully crafted, melodic pieces with poetic, often stirring lyrics about everyday life and common experiences.

Likely the earliest — and most threatened — of the ancient music forms is *arek*, best translated as 'spirit', rooted in animistic beliefs and performed to communicate with the ghosts of diseased ancestors. Sadly, the skills needed to

Early pin peat orchestra

perform *arek* are dying with the musicians who practise them.

Weddings and funerals each have their respective, ages-old music and songs, the latter performed by a *pin peat* ensemble. Khmer nuptial celebrations are large-scale affairs that can traditionally last up to a week but which are more realistically, not to mention affordably, truncated to a maximum of three days. *Pleng khar*, or wedding music (*pleng* means 'music' in Khmer) is an essential part of the marriage rites, played throughout the festivities though often recorded rather than live, and features instruments that include the *tro*, *khloy* and *skor* plus male and female singers.

These days it's not just traditional music that issues loudly from the marquees typically set up to host wedding parties, and the pop favourites most likely to get guests on their feet — and to the ubiquitous karaoke mic — are the 'old songs', the Golden Age classics.

For centuries the music heard across Cambodia was exclusively of the ancient order. Around mid to late 19th century, western-style music began to infiltrate the country and it did so in a circuitous way, from Manila.

King Norodom Prohmbarirak, monarch from 1860 to 1904, became enamoured of the military bands favoured by the courts of Europe and elsewhere and imported a brace of Filipino musicians to expand his personal roster of musical talent. With them they brought trombones, oboes, flutes and clarinets, instruments previously unheard in the Kingdom. The compositions they played, and which they taught to pupils, were initially royal fanfares and marches, later augmented with western string instruments to include orchestral pieces.

Also at court were the King's own troupe of traditional musicians, handpicked from the finest in the country to perform for the royal family and their elite guests. The palace became a sonic melting pot of ancient and modern, western and Khmer from which a distinctive hybrid would emerge.

The rise of what became known as 'modern' or 'new' music found an audience more than willing to appreciate and assimilate foreign influences and styles — particularly if they could dance to them. The popular beats were frequently of Latin origin; the tango, mambo, samba and cha-cha-cha. Before long they overflowed the rarified circles of the rich and powerful and swept the regular citizens of Phnom Penh onto their feet and into the new dance clubs that were springing up. By the 1930s and 40s the floodgates to contemporary western music were open. Foreign musical films began to be screened in towns and cities, where the arrival of the gramophone brought with it new opportunities for urbanites to enjoy the popular songs. Meanwhile, in the Cambodian countryside, touring *lckhorn* theatre troupes were introducing western wind and string instruments into their productions, alerting their audiences to the foreign sounds alive in the capital and elsewhere.

In 1946 the National School of Music was established in Phnom Penh and incorporated in 1965 within the Royal University of Fine Arts. Students were tutored in both Traditional Khmer and classical European music, learning musical theory and notation. Prior to the 20th century, Khmer music and songs had been handed down simply by playing from memory. Around 1913 the King's Director of Music, a Frenchman named Francois Perruchot, had introduced musical notation to the country, allowing palace musicians to read and perform music from abroad and to record on paper their own classical pieces.

Ever the enthusiastic patron of the arts, Sihanouk continued the palace's practice of maintaining a royal orchestra made up of the most eminent performers and singers of the day, who would travel alongside him on provincial tours to perform songs that praised the beauty of the locations they visited. He encouraged his ministries to form their own musical groups, which became the launch pads for the careers of many of the country's popular singing stars.

When rock and roll was unleashed on the western world in the late 1950s, a corner of the East was ready and waiting.

Twists...

In the late 1950s, art student Chum Kem left his native Cambodia for Italy to take up a scholarship in Ceramics. Kem's pursuits abroad clearly extended beyond his studies. While there he won a talent contest, made several Italian language pop records, appeared in the 1960 musical film, *Un Mandarino per Teo* and returned home in 1962, a famous pop star, bearing a gift that would quickly sweep the country's dance clubs: the

Artist-turned-twister
Chum Kem

Kampuchea Twist. All the rage in the west, where critics had also initially slammed it as provocative, the twist proved even more controversial in the Kingdom. Its energetic contortions could hardly differ more from the slow, serene steps and graceful hand movements of Khmer traditional dance; how could such ugly, unrefined locomotions even be referred to as dancing? 'Is it an art? Is it a sport? Is it a healthy pastime?' These questions were posed by French language newspaper, *La Depeche du Cambodge*, surviving copies of which are held in the Cambodian national archives, and hotly debated by readers on the letters page.

Despite these divided opinions, the twist took off in a big way in the Kingdom's dance clubs and spawned a spate of follow-up records, like Pan Ron's *Dance the Twist*, equally geared towards twisting the night away.

...and turns

On 15 April 2015, Khmer New Year, 2,015 dancers gathered in Angkor National Park to set a new world record. They were there, in a setting better known for the depiction of traditional *apsara* dancers on the ancient walls of Angkor Wat, to break the Guinness world record for the largest madison, a dance craze that arrived in Cambodia in the 1960s from America. Khmer people took this insinuatingly contagious line dance with its deftly-executed kick-turn so firmly to their hearts that it remains a staple at wedding parties alongside the more traditional *romvong*, or circle dancing (*rom* meaning 'dance' in Khmer). In fact any social gathering where the appropriate music is played — Ros Sereysothea's *Old Pot Still Makes Good Rice* is one example — will likely witness a spontaneous madison outbreak.

FIVE

The First Guitar Heroes

'The new dance beat has arrived ... get up and dance, dance, dance.'

Voa Saroun, *A New Dance Beat*

Cambodian society had for decades been absorbing European culture. Between 1863 and 1953 the country rested less than easily within the French protectorate known as Indochina, of which Vietnam and Laos were also part. Following Independence it remained home to a sizeable ex-pat French community and travel between the countries was commonplace. Among the items that made their way into the Kingdom from Europe were vinyl records, at first mainly jazz and recordings by artists like Edith Piaf and Tino Rossi, and later western rock and roll and pop music.

Phnom Penh had no shortage of accomplished young musicians, many tutored at the royal palace or the university's school of music, and the adventurous among them were keen to experiment with the new beats infiltrating the country from abroad. Guitars, particularly the electric variety, were the way to go and the capital's embryonic rockers were eager to get their hands on the newest, coolest instruments. Guitar groups — or yé-yé groups as they were known after the French appellation — formed and flourished. By the 1960s Royal Cambodian Radio was taking notice. Western-style pop music began permeating not just the capital's party and nightclub scene but the national airwaves too. Suddenly it seemed no song was complete without a solid bass line and some juicy guitar licks. The Kingdom's music fans were grooving to a new sound; charged, idiosyncratic.

There were no rules to follow, or to break, in the Kingdom's nascent rock scene. No real genres to speak of just new dance crazes to accompany as Latin standards like the cha-cha-cha and bolero, and traditional favourites like the *sarawan* moved over to accommodate the twist, the madison, the monkey, the jerk and the a-go-go in the country's lexicon of popular dance. For Khmer youth, pop music was not the stuff of revolution or even rebellion, just something to enjoy. Young people were, and to a large extent still are, accustomed to respect the system and their elders, not to kick against them.

Rhythm and blues psychedelia, surf rock, the already well-established Latin grooves and a sprinkling of saccharine pop; all found their way into the mix, not infrequently within the same song. Khmer musicians took this heady brew of influences and served it up with a dash of eastern spice to produce a sound that still feels remarkably fresh and vital. A riot of distorted guitars, Farfisa organ, drums and sometimes brass, frequently overlaid with ethereally high-pitched female vocals that combined to evoke the raw energy of 1960s American garage bands coupled with early Tamla Motown.

Cambodia's musicians, singers and songwriters did not so much appropriate western music as customise it freely and expressively to synthesise a new and distinctive genre that would prove, against the most tragic of odds, remarkably enduring.

Baksey Cham Krong pictured performing at Battambang College (Mol Kagnol centre guitar)

For Baksey Cham Krong, named after a temple in the ancient Angkor complex and hailed as Cambodia's first guitar band, making music was a family affair. The group's first line up started out in 1945 performing traditional *mahori* music with western instruments: Mol Samoth on banjo, Mol Samin on acoustic guitar and Mol Sa Mel on violin, with Mol Kamach joining his brothers on vocals at the tender age of six.

'My brothers recorded a few dozen songs on the national radio,' recalls affable veteran guitarman Mol Kagnol. 'My father ordered a number of them on 78 rpm records for family use but none of them survived. The band was dismantled when my three older brothers got day jobs.' It was the mid-1950s and Kagnol, by then in his early teens, was impatient to follow in their footsteps and knew exactly the music he wanted to make — and the look to go with it.

'I was listening to mambo, cha-cha-cha, waltz, tango, The Platters, Bill Haley, Pat Boon and Paul Anka and I watched Elvis movies. But the two bands that opened the door to my heart and were relevant to us Cambodians were The Ventures and Cliff Richard and The Shadows. Modern music was already in Cambodia at that time, but it was the big band style, too complicated for me. I wanted a guitar band instead.'

Kagnol put together Baksey Cham Krong mark two with his bass-playing cousin, Oeur Sam Ol, whose father was a well-known film actor. Mol Kamach joined them on vocals and quickly acquired local heart throb status. They became, in Kagnol's words, 'sharp-suited siblings – the Cliff Richard and The Shadows of Cambodia.'

Mol Kagnol (right) with bandmates (left to right): Hong Samley; Mol Kamach and Oeur Sam Ol (in background)

Reluctant to see their teenage sons let loose on the town, the Mol parents built a stage and dance floor in the family's sizeable yard where they played open air shows for few hundred-strong crowds of friends and family, the first venue in Cambodia to host music for young yé-yé fans. The band even started its own fan club: 'It was somewhat prestigious to be a Baksey member,' Kagnol smiles.

In mid-1950s Cambodia it took more than ability and enthusiasm to make rock music. Guitars were extremely hard to come by and a certain ingenuity — with electrical skills an advantage — was required to furnish a band with the necessary equipment. In Britain at that time, cash-strapped musicians were using improvised and home-made instruments to revive the early 20th century American music known as skiffle. The Mol brothers were from a wealthy silversmith family, it was not money that was the problem, as Kagnol explains:

'There was only one store, called Panabou [a sports retailer located near Psar Tney, also known as Central Market, Panabou became the first shop in Phnom Penh to sell records and musical instruments] and they had just one guitar for sale. We tried to make our own equipment, we made a one string bass out of a gasoline can and a broomstick and I made an electric guitar out of a square microphone with rubber band plugged into the radio'.

The band's first electric bass required some outside help. 'I talked to a carpenter next door who made wooden model shoes for a shoemaker downtown,' remembers Kagnol, 'I told him, "If you can carve wooden shoes you can carve me a solid body guitar too." He accepted the challenge and my brother number four, Mol Sa Em [an electronics whiz who, usefully, owned an electrical shop], and I built the electronic part.

'The next instrument I built was a twelve string guitar, a copy of a guitar I saw on the cover of a Shadows album. I had no idea what brand name or model but I know now it was a Vox guitar from the UK. I took apart a Hofner guitar in order to build this one. We never owned a drum kit, we borrowed or rented one.'

The band were, however, the proud possessors of a Gibson amp from the USA, a gift from Kagnol's father when his son completed elementary school that cost 27,000 riels in local currency, the price of a motor scooter!

Baksey Cham Krong's guitar-driven beat was a revelation to Phnom Penh's young set who seized upon this new sound so distinct from the more established rhythms their parents enjoyed. As the band's fame and fan base grew, its gigs became more prestigious, at major hotels and the houses of governors and diplomats. In 1960 the band made its television breakthrough on the hugely popular show, *National Congress*.

'We ended up with five guitars on stage', remembers Kagnol. 'I wanted only three guitarists but I didn't know how to fire the other two. The next day it was the big story in town: the first guitar band in Cambodia. And I saw some kid with a broomstick in his hand pretending he was playing guitar. I realised then the influence I was making. After that, guitar bands were popping up like mushrooms. If it was not me that started it up it would be somebody else or a few more years later. The energy was there for the Cambodian yé-yé generation.'

Baksey fans were only too happy to add home grown recordings to their collections and snapped up the band's records on 78 rpm. Sales of its biggest hit, *Adios Maman* (reissued in 2016 on the French Akuphone label), written by Mol Samin before he headed off to college in Paris, rivalled those of *Champa Battambang (Flower of Battambang)* the top selling record by Cambodia's number one singing star, Sin Sisamouth. So popular was the song that Sisamouth himself asked the band's permission to record his own version. His request, Kagnol says, was very politely refused as, 'We dedicated this song to mom and dad, it was too personal to let it get out of the family.'

Original record sleeve featuring Baksey heart-throb Mol Kamach

In 1966 the Mol brothers decided to draw a line under their band career when college beckoned. The rock music they had kickstarted would roll on without them. Their last gig took Baksey Cham Krong full circle back to Sisowath High School where their live career began. 'That was our best performance,' Kagnol reflects, 'I played my new twelve-string guitar and the keyboard at same time.'

Where Baksey had never intended to be anything other than an amateur band, the next generation of guitar groups would be able to make a living from their music. Baksey's guitarist Hong Samley and drummer Loeurn Landy went on to form the Bayon Band while rhythm guitarist Him Craven joined Apsara. Formed in 1960 by a bunch of students at the university, the latter won a national talent contest and had the distinction of a bona-fide royal on keyboards. The multi-instrumentalist Prince Panara Sirivuth also co-wrote the band's original songs including *Goddess of Kep* and *When I First Met You*, recorded in 1964 on the Wat Phnom label.

Baksey bassist Oeur Sam Ol was later sponsored by the Mol family to attend music school. The only Baksey member to receive formal musical training, he became a professor of music at the university and, in the 1970s, the leader of a republican army band. Only three band members, Kagnol, Kamach and Hong Samley, survived the Khmer Rouge genocide. Kamach and Samley settled in Paris while a turn of events took Kagnol to the US.

Some five months before Phnom Penh fell to the Khmer Rouge, and by then with a degree in structural engineering under his belt, Kagnol was given the opportunity to train as a test pilot on a US airbase. The move to America saved his life but April 1975 saw him stuck in America with no news of his family in Cambodia and sick with worry about their fate:

'Suddenly Cambodia was like a black hole, nothing was getting out. The Pentagon gave me thirty days notice to get out of their airbase, with three options: I can stay in the USA as a refugee and apply for political asylum; if I want to go to a third country, they can officially send me there. If I want to go back to Cambodia, they will send me to China and let the Chinese do the rest. Only China has any contact with Cambodia [at this point].

'I can no longer access the family bank account, all systems have been destroyed. I've got no money, no job. I'm no longer a cool test pilot, I've no degree, not even a high school diploma, nothing useful any more as America did not recognise any of my qualifications as legitimate'.

But Kagnol possessed one skill that the USA did value: the ability to play kick-ass rock and roll. After a helpful introduction, the manager of an officers' club on the airbase gave him $250 upfront to buy a guitar and the Khmer Hank Marvin was back in business, playing rock, country music, top 40 hits and surf guitar by night and driving a delivery truck by day. In five years the resourceful Kagnol had financed another round of higher education, this time in English rather than French, and paid a second — though not, as it turns out, final — farewell to the music business.

Now in his 70s and living in Phoenix, Arizona, Kagnol muses on the way his life has unfolded:

'Ironically, the thing that my family culture does not agree with turns out to be really useful for me. I still remember my father laughing and saying, "you were born in the wrong country, you like engineering stuff, you like rock and roll, you can't make it in Cambodia with that." '

In the mid-1970s Kagnol was reunited with his brother Kamach, who was living in Paris, and the pair recorded an album. Six years later he underwent major heart surgery and was ready to consider his live music career over — but US film maker John Pirozzi had other ideas.

Promoting his documentary film about Cambodian music, *Don't Think I've Forgotten* (covered in Chapter 12), Pirozzi invited the musicians he'd met during filming to play a series of gigs in the US. The short tour also took them — most poignantly for the local audience — to the gardens of

Phnom Penh's Chaktomuk Theatre for the film's Cambodian premiere in January 2014. Kagnol and Kamach were part of this supergroup along with members of Bayon and Drakkcr bands. The elder statesmen of Khmer rock were back in the spotlight, blasting new life into the greatest hits of their youth.

SIX

In Their Own Words

*'Dance, dance, dance, it's never enough.
I want to dance till morning.'*

Pan Ron, *Dance, Dance, Dance*

The 1960s found the Kingdom of Wonder grooving in a uniquely Cambodian way. The hunger for music and dancing in the capital and elsewhere spurred the eventual rise of a thriving local recording industry. Thousands of new songs were written and recorded for labels like Wat Phnom, Angkor, Apsara, Kampuchea, Independence, Chanchhaya, Monorom and Bokor. Despite the efforts of a small number of enthusiasts to research, collect and catalogue, it's impossible to know how many were produced but there's no doubt the output was immensely prolific. One song book publisher recalls a book of 500 songs recorded by one artist alone, the 'Emperor of Khmer Pop', singer Sin Sisamouth, who

would almost certainly have sold at least as many to other publishing houses.

Though the country had its share of hardworking original songwriters — Voy Ho, Mer Bun, Oum Dara and Svay Sam Eua are among those credited on surviving record sleeves — Cambodian recording artists also borrowed freely from their western counterparts and had no qualms about tinkering with the source material.

Among the mixed bag of songs that received this Khmer-style makeover, rendering them teasingly familiar yet sufficiently alien to elicit a double-take from the western listener, are The Beatles' *Hard Day's Night*; *Venus*, the Shocking Blue chart topper; and Sonny and Cher's hit *Bang Bang*. It's unknown if any of the original artists or songwriters were aware of these mutated covers let alone what they would have made of them. Certainly the relevant copyrights were never acknowledged nor, presumably, were any royalties paid.

While the rhythms of western rock and pop songs had a universal appeal, the words, if they were even understood, were not so relatable. Matters of the heart may be common currency in the world of popular music but some of the more particular concerns of freewheeling western youth must have failed to resonate quite so strongly in a country bypassed by the new, permissive society of the 1960s and where life outside the capital still carried on in a relatively simple, traditional fashion. The solution for Cambodia's musicians and songwriters was straightforward: they simply composed new sets of lyrics in their own language that reflected the culture familiar to their audience.

The subject matter was invariably romance, heartbreak and an often playful battle of the sexes; a litany of love, loss and separation, with anguish experienced on both sides of the gender divide. The lyrical landscape was usually bucolic, recalling earlier folk ballads, sometimes involving a nostalgia-tinged pride in a particular city or province.

In the hands of Khmer rocker Yol Aularong, Them's anthemic *Gloria* loses its spelt-out chorus to become the more innocent yet still raucously powerful *Broken-Hearted Bachelor*. Where Van Morrison racks up the sexual tension as his girlfriend approaches, knocks on his door, climbs up his stairs to ultimately makes him 'feel alright', Aularong complains:

'I'm a broken-hearted bachelor, fooled about a girl's intentions.
I loved her each and every day, then she went and got married.'

Sin Sisamouth's version of the traditional blues classic *House of the Rising Sun* is chronologically switched to *Sunset* (the song is also well-known as *I'm Still Waiting*), its time-honoured theme of thwarted passion far removed from any New Orleans house of ill repute:

'The sun is setting – where are you my love? ... I'm still waiting for you.
Tomorrow I'll say goodbye. Come, my love, let's spend the night together
For tomorrow I'll be gone far away from you and I don't know when we'll meet again.'

Image courtesy CVMA

Though probably best known internationally as a hit for The Animals, the song was also covered by French crooner Johnny Hallyday as *Le Penitencier*, again with completely different rather than merely translated lyrics. Hallyday himself was no stranger to contrafactum — the process of substituting the lyrics of a song with another set while keeping more or less the same music — and it may well have been this version that Cambodians were more familiar with.

Sisamouth's *Missing Tender Hands* may be more familiar as Scott McKenzie's *San Francisco*, though its lyrics, as in many of the singer's poetically sentimental ballads, are more doomed romance than hippy love-in:

"Remembering and dreaming of your words.
When we used to talk, just the two of us.
Deep in the night, watching the dark moon."

Fleetwood Mac's *Black Magic Woman* is equally transformed by Sisamouth, with a treatment clearly influenced by the Santana cover, into *I Love Petite Women*:

'A sharp, fine nose; curvy, tiny waist ... may I dance with you or may I not?'

Listeners might well spot a strong resemblance between Sereysothea's *Cry Loving Me* and the Creedence Clearwater Revival song *Proud Mary*, popularly covered by Ike and Tina Turner. The original extols the freedom of life on a Mississippi riverboat away from the rat race; Sereysothea, however, anchors the song firmly in the familiar territory of unrequited love with the lines:

> 'I'm very flattered because I know some men have a crush on me, but I act annoyed instead. Some cry because of love.'

While the chorus exchanges the familiar line about rolling on a river for:

> 'Love, love, cry because of love.'

Indeed the vagaries of romantic love, a rich source of inspiration in any songwriting culture, form the basis of most of the Golden Age singers' original repertoires too, sometimes despairing, as in *When Will We Be Married?*, also by Sereysothea:

> 'My love what are you waiting for?
> If you are in love with another girl
> I will go on a hunger strike and kill myself,'

sometimes provocative, like *One Glass Of Wine* performed by the same singer:

> 'Darling, I give you a glass of wine, please taste it ... you're intoxicated, but not from the wine. The wine tastes delicious, but not as delicious as me.'

References to physical love, we can see, were perhaps not as overt as they might have been in the west at the time and were often cloaked in innuendo.

Image courtesy CVMA

Khmer culture holds female modesty in high regard. In Khmer song, as in real life, the girl's virtue was closely guarded and not to be trifled with. Female vocalists warned their suitors against playing fast and loose with their feelings. Though the lyrics are commonly fraught with despair, the melodies are frequently up tempo and highly danceable. It's noteworthy but unsurprising that the vast majority, if not all of these songs were penned by men.

Though young women were wary of unwanted attentions they certainly knew how to tease their admirers.

In Ros Sereysothea's *New Year's Day*, the protagonist makes it clear that at 15 she's not ready for a boyfriend:

'It's the start of a New Year, the start of womanhood. My body has changed dramatically.

> Men all check me out, but I'm just not interested ... I'm waiting ten months longer.'

While, in what sounds like the perfect follow-up, *I'm Sixteen*, the same singer asserts confidently:

> 'I'm sixteen. So free of worries. Life is like a flower, spreading perfume everywhere,"

as male voices respond eagerly, asking for her love.

Pan Ron exemplified a new breed of Cambodian womanhood, at least in terms of her image as a singer; freer, fun loving, in keeping with the independent spirit of the Golden Age. In *There's Nothing To Be Ashamed Of*, she revels in the sensations of new love:

> 'Love is so sweet. Oh, it's killing me!
> Oh, love is sweeter than honey.
> ... My mind is blank, oh my body is floating.
> I'm so hot it's like I'm on fire.'

And in *Chills to My Spine* declares in forthright manner:

> 'If I can't have you I will never be warm.'

Though the sentiments of the Houy Meas Song *Unique Child* appear at odds with the feminist movement then sweeping the western world, viewed within its cultural and religious context the song paints a quite compelling portrait of female strength and stoicism:

'A mother cries, a mother screams, a mother calls promising her love.
She waits and waits, she will always wait for her child's father.
Please stop asking about your father. He is a womaniser and an embarrassment.
This is karma from our past lives, you just have to accept it.'

Indeed women in song may often be wronged, but they are rarely pushovers and have their menfolk sussed. In another of her songs, Pan Ron has a stern warning for a would-be suitor:

'If you are honest you don't need to swear to prove you are single — and don't think I don't know ... don't try to flirt with me ... if you are in a hurry to buy milk for your kids, go ahead. Don't follow me ... bye bye.'

Nor is Ros Sereysothea fooled by her wayward spouse in *Wicked Husband*:

> 'He's quiet and so still at home.
> The moment he's out of the house his personality and attitude changes.
> Eyes open wide, checking out girls without any shame ...
> Watch out, when you get home I'll teach you a lesson.'

It's not just women, though, who are wronged in Khmer song. Men too regularly experienced heartbreak at the hands of absent or cold-hearted lovers. In *Still Not Enough*, Sin Sisamouth agonises:

> 'I'm so true to you ... why do you still betray me? I tried to take good care of you, never to displease you yet still you break my heart.'

While in *Nevertheless* he appears more resigned:

> *'I must try hard to forget you. If I die, I'm fine with that.'*

Khmer people love their food and in Cambodia rice has a cultural importance beyond that of a mere culinary staple, so it's of little surprise that food analogies were an ingredient of many a popular song. Lyrics commonly describe the qualities of love as 'sweet and sour' as in *Oh Love*, by Ros Sereysothea:

> *'Since I've grown up and become mature*
> *I've not known the meaning of love.*
> *What does it taste like, should I long for it or not?*
> *Bland or sweet, sour or salty?'*

In An *Old Pot Still Makes Good Rice*, the same singer tells her errant husband:

> *'If you come back I'll welcome you.*
> *We'll start a new chapter of our lives.*
> *The old pot still cooks the rice you once enjoyed.*
> *Eaten day or night, the rice is always warm.'*

In the west, the 1960s was a time of revolution, with music a natural vehicle for the protest movement. In Cambodia music was for dancing to, not for advocating change, and songs about dancing were as popular as the dancing itself. Sin Sisamouth's *Learn How to Dance the Monkey* and Voa Saroun's *A New Dance Beat* were among the numbers that enticed the audience onto the dance floor, along with Pan

Ron's *Dance A-go-go, Dance, Dance, Dance,* and *Monkey Dancing the Monkey*:

> 'I saw a monkey doing the monkey dance.
> The monkey was so smart there was nothing to compare ...
> Making funny faces and laughing out loud.'

Ros Sereysothea interprets Sam the Sham's worldwide dance hit *Woolly Bully* (a song itself adapted from earlier recorded material) as *Wolly Polly*. The lyrics are changed but the exhortation to dance remains:

> 'We dance for fun.
> We dance with the band ...
> Please dance as you wish'.

If Cambodian pop music was no place for political comment, its fans certainly enjoyed a touch of social satire, notably in the hands of comedy singers like Meas Samoun. In *The Engagement*, Samoun makes fun of the intensive vetting process by his prospective in-laws:

> 'What was I expected to say?
> Questioned as if I was in court.
> The food smelled so delicious but I was too busy trying to be polite.
> Starving as I was I didn't get a bite to eat'.

In *Finding a Wife in the Provinces*, which he performs with Sin Sisamouth, the duo compare their unsuccessful attempts to find a suitable partner in every Cambodian province, before finally vying for the attentions of a beautiful Battambang girl and coming to verbal blows:

> 'If I have her as my wife we'll make a good couple'.
> 'No you won't, you're too old.'
> 'Nonsense she suits me better than you.'
> 'Eh? Your face is full of ringworm. Don't bother to ask for her hand they won't give it to you.'

Singer and guitarist, Yol Aularong was probably the least conformist of his peer group, with a taste for rowdy rock and roll, low-down blues and offbeat lyrics with a humorous, often satirical bent. His self-penned songs range from the cocky bravado of *Cyclo*:

> 'Riding a cyclo to central Market.
> Checking out girls wearing those maternity blouses.
> Thought she was pregnant but she's not, it's just the new fashion.
> Every day I ride a cyclo and check out girls
> If I'm poor because of it, that's OK.'

To *Whiskey Whiskey*, a bluesy, belligerent toast to heavy drinking that laments,

> 'When I drink too much my insides turn rotten.
> Treating with medicine is no help at all.'

Gender rules

Generations of Khmer women have been brought up in the shadow of the *Chbab Srey*, or 'Rules for Women'. The now-controversial and increasingly out-dated code of conduct remained part of the educational curriculum well into the 2010s. Taking the form of a lengthy piece of verse, composed towards the end of the 19th century by the late, much-venerated Khmer poet Krom Ngoy, it is still taught in some schools, if only as classic literature. The oeuvre counsels women to be of good character, to work hard, defer to their husbands and show respect and gratitude to their parents. Women are warned not to bring outside problems into the home or to discuss domestic problems with outsiders. They should be gentle and modest in their demeanour, stepping lightly and speaking in a quiet voice, hence the stillness of manner and elegance of movement that epitomises the Khmer female ideal.

And, yes, there is a code for men too. The *Chbab Proh* encourages the man of the house to be hard-working, measured in his actions, polite and non-aggressive and to consider his wife and family when making financial decisions. It also includes a stern rebuke against 'madness' with gambling, women and alcohol.

An ancient Khmer saying, however, reveals a belief that still persists today. 'Men are like gold, women are like cloth' reads the translation, meaning that men's misdemeanours can be wiped away whereas women's leave an indelible stain on their reputation.

A case of mistaken identity?

In the late 1960s and early 1970s Voy Ho was a well known figure on the music scene, a prolific writer of hugely popular songs including a good many of Sin Sisamouth's hits, whose output would have put his famously productive counterparts in Manhattan's Brill Building to shame. But like so many of his Cambodian contemporaries, Voy Ho perished during the Khmer Rouge period.

Voy Ho in the 60s

Or did he? In 2012 a man claiming to be Ho surfaced in rural Battambang and took part in a controversial interview on Cambodian TV. Conveniently perhaps, the re-materialised Ho, by then in his early 80s, was disfigured facially making it harder to compare his appearance with that of the much younger man, of whom some photos have survived.

Was this the real Voy Ho? The jury is still out. After his TV appearance many people declared him an imposter. Indeed the surviving family members interviewed were unconvinced. But in Battambang where he now lives, writing songs for $5 a pop, many locals are content to believe he is the real deal.

Whatever the truth, the episode illustrates the shadowy area between fact, fallacy and a desire to forget a painful past that often lurks frustratingly, if understandably, around Cambodia's recent history.

SEVEN

Rocking the Boat

*'They say I've fallen under your love spell,
but I'm just crazy loving you.'*

Drakkar, *Crazy Loving You*

When Touch Seang Tana's mother bought him his first guitar, a smart new Yamaha acoustic, the budding musician promised her faithfully he would only play it as a hobby. Little could she know her teenage son would go on to front the band, Drakkar, Cambodia's best-selling rock group of its time.

Tana, now a senior government official and an amiable and entertaining raconteur, had a strict upbringing. 'My family was an educated family,' he explains, 'they wanted me to be a scientist or something like that, not to play music.' The guitar in question, one of the first Yamaha models to hit Cambodia, was in fact a reward for his academic achievements bought with severe parental misgivings and the princely cash sum of 10,000 Cambodian riels — more than double a teacher's monthly salary.

'If you didn't have the money to buy, the shop owner wouldn't even let you touch the guitars,' he remembers. 'They had cheaper guitars for around 4,000 to 5,000 riels and Vietnamese guitars were cheap, I think you could buy them for 300 or 400 riels.

The Drakkar band took shape in 1967, the result of a chance meeting outside a Phnom Penh record shop, one of a couple in the capital that carried western records. A mutual friend introduced Tana to Touch Chhattha (no relation), who borrowed some of the vinyl his new acquaintance had just bought. Within days the pair had put together a band with Chhattha's friend Mam Molivan on bass.

Chhattha and Molivan were in their twenties and already experienced players in the music scene that had by then engulfed the capital and captured the imagination of young people eager for fun, fame and, according to Tana, the alluringly sophisticated French girls who frequented the top dance clubs. Tana just 16 at the time, could barely play guitar but was not about to let that deter his ambitions.

'They knew how to play songs by many British and American bands. Me, I knew just one song, *Walking The Dog*,' he admits, 'I was very shy to play in front of them. I played Chhattha's [acoustic] guitar and just followed what he played. Molivan sang lead vocals and I started harmonising with him.

'At the time all the bands were playing the same songs, famous songs from the British hit parade by The Beatles and The Rolling Stones. You would go to a party and hear the same song played five times by five different bands. But in '67 The Bee Gees' music invaded Cambodia and they became more important than The Beatles and The Rolling Stones.'

Caption - Drakkar's 1970s line-up (left to right): Touch Chhattha; Som Sareth (seated); Ouk Sam Ath; Touch Seang Tana

Tana introduced his fellow band members to his neighbour Tan Panareth, also 16, who could, says Tana, sing like Robin Gibb:

'His parents were also very strict but they trusted my family and let him come with me. Panareth sang the Bee Gees songs. My voice was like Mick Jagger's so I sang all the Rolling Stones songs.'

Beatles numbers were covered by Molivan, whose McCartney-esque vocals and bass guitar earned him the nickname Mr Paul. To find the lyrics the band regularly scoured the pages of a French music magazine, *Salut Les Copains*, which printed the words to the latest hits in English. Recruiting a drummer proved problematic; the best were already busy with club dates every night of the week so the band settled for bringing in whoever was available for its gigs.

Within a week the newly-formed Drakkar, sometimes spelt Thra Ka and named after a Viking longship, had its first live outing standing in for a friend's band. The gig was a high-profile one, a costume party at Phnom Penh's upmarket Cirque Sportif, near Wat Phnom where the US embassy now stands, a venue favoured by rich students from the city's Lycée Descartes.

Tana describes the scene: 'My mother gave us 500 riels to go to the market to buy costumes. We arrived in a *cyclo* [a bicycle rickshaw]. Five people in a *cyclo*! The security staff were surprised, people didn't arrive at Cirque Sportif by *cyclo*, they arrived by car. The first thing I saw was Prince Norodom Sirivuth, [of Kroeusna Band], dressed like a *matelot*, singing and playing piano. The others all knew him and shook his hand. I was a bit shy and not very happy; no one knew me and no one shook my hand.'

Tana had never even held an electric guitar let alone played one until he set foot on the Cirque Sportif stage. In mid-sixties Cambodia electric guitars were a luxury few young musicians could afford for themselves. A common practice was for bands to hire the instruments they needed for each gig from the shops that sold them while the venues themselves provided amplifiers along with other sound equipment. Baksey Cham Krong, he remembers, were the only band that owned all its own equipment.

Drakkar's first number was the Bee Gees song *The Singer Sang His Song*. 'Everyone was so quiet, no one was talking, they stopped dancing. Then Molivan sang Lennon and McCartney's *Michelle*. What a voice, all the French girls came over to the stage. We thought, how can he do this, we've only rehearsed three or four times? It was our first show but after that everyone knew us, everyone talked about the Drakkar. We may not have been the best musicians but we had the best vocalists.'

In the mid to late 1960s, for the middle and upper classes at least, the weekend was party time and Drakkar became the band most-wanted to play those parties. Tana, who became the band's decision-maker in such matters, decided they would be selective about the dates they accepted. The exclusivity only increased their popularity, plus he was able to reassure his mother he was playing for fun, not for a living.

'In those days you had a lot of freedom,' he recalls, 'you could do whatever you wanted. Everyone enjoyed life, it was a wonderful time. On one weekend night there would be at least ten parties.'

Indeed, according to Tana, Phnom Penh's nightlife was prolific, with some thirty to forty venues catering to middle class Cambodians with live music and dancing. Some of the most popular venues were operated by the state-owned retail chain, Magasin D'Etat: the Chaktomuk Floating Nightclub and the Pochentong Dancing Bar, the latter located by the airport and where some of the top musicians played. Two or three up-scale French-style clubs were the preserve of the upper classes where the music of choice was jazz played on piano and saxophone. At weekends, less affluent young music lovers would flock to *Veal Preah Man*, a park by the royal palace, where a stage would be erected and the site more formally used for the annual Ploughing Festival and other state events would be given over to music, dancing and the opportunity to hang out with friends.

Some of the major provincial cities had their own live music scenes too, most notably the country's second city, Battambang, and its major seaport, Kampong Saom, today more familiarly known as Sihanoukville. The latter boasted upwards of twenty nightclubs that catered to passengers and crew on the ships that docked there as well as to locals.

But the parties would not last, and not only for Drakkar. As the 1960s drew to a close the band was growing apart and finally broke up. In 1970 Norodom Sihanouk's culturally liberal government yielded, under force and with US backing, to the new more restrictive Khmer Republic. Society was changing and with it the country's music industry. Vinyl records gave way to cheaper and easier to produce cassette recordings and Chinese-owned companies began to corner the market in their production, distribution and sales. The country so at home with European culture was now increasingly susceptible to American influence.

The US was at war across the Cambodian border in Vietnam. Indeed, it had crossed that border (and, for many, crossed an ethical line) with its aerial bombardment of the so-called Ho

Chi Minh trail used by the Vietnamese to move troops and supplies from North to South Vietnam. An action that had in part supported the rise of Pol Pot. On the American domestic front the anti-war movement was growing. Cambodia had a civil war of its own underway but for the inhabitants of Phnom Penh, unaccustomed to public protest, popular unrest amounted to little more than a refusal to give up the entertainment they enjoyed. When evening curfews were introduced following a spate of bombings in the capital, cinemas took to showing films during the day and musicians switched their shows to the afternoon.

In 1971, with some personnel changes and a more casual format now its members were busy with their careers, Drakkar reformed to play a tour of US military training camps in Southern Vietnam. The new line up of Tana on rhythm guitar, Som Sareth on lead, drummer Ouk Sam Ath and bass player Oeur Sam Ol, with the later addition of returning guitarist Touch Chhattha, had a harder, edgier sound that reflected changing musical tastes.

For decades Latin beats had underpinned the rhythm of Cambodian popular music and in the 1970s the highly percussive Latin fusion of the American rock band Santana caught the imagination of Khmer rock fans. Tana, by now working as a programme director for the national radio station, switched to keyboards and the band introduced congas and timbale. 'People liked our music,' he says, 'because when we played live we played like Santana, with lots of percussion.'

Eventually Drakkar was coaxed into the studio owned by the Mol brothers, formerly of Baksey Cham Krong of which Oeur Sam Ol had been a member, where they produced the material for their first album. The band members decided to sidestep the Chinese companies, with whom Tana had already worked on a series of multi-artist cassettes, and put the album out themselves, a labour-intensive task that involved physically copying and labelling each cassette. Sales were slow — the Chinese had no interest in promoting albums in their stores that they had not also produced — and four months on a mere 100 copies had been shifted. Disillusioned, Tana left Phnom Penh for Pailin near the Thai border to take up a promising business opportunity.

Out of the blue, a phone call from the capital brought surprising news that quickly turned his focus back to the album. Every copy had been sold. More cassettes were produced as a matter of urgency and flew off the shelves, racking up sales of over 30,000. It was February 1975, Tana and his bandmates had Cambodia's top-selling album to date on their hands and were ready to capitalise on its success.

Surprise hit: an original Drakkar cassette

A success that would, sadly, be short-lived.

On 17 April 1975 Khmer Rouge troops captured and evacuated Phnom Penh. The music was over and so was life as Cambodian people had known it.

Like most of his fellow musicians, Tana tried desperately to hide his background from Khmer Rouge military. The ability to convince them he was a peasant performer rather than an educated, middle class artist meant the difference between life and death. Although, as many of the militia were teenagers and young men who were rock fans themselves, his talents also bought unlikely protection, as he explains:

'One soldier asked me many questions about the old times. He asked me if I knew how to play guitar and if I knew how to play "imperialist" [American] songs'. Tana was only too aware of the danger — the Khmer Rouge tolerated only patriotic, propagandist songs, the punishment for even whistling a 'decadent' western song was dire — but he had no choice. 'I played for his group for about five minutes. He said "Don't worry, brother, no-one will touch you." He protected me for a short period of time but afterwards he moved on, then I was in danger again.'

Every one of Tana's siblings and the majority of his former band mates — only Touch Chhattha and Ouk Sam Ath survived the regime — perished under the communists, leaving Tana at a loss to explain his own survival: 'They go to kill me many times ... again and again I got lucky. I was seriously sick, I was in a coma, but I survived'.

Today Tana is still mak ng music and Drakkar's album is once more picking up sales. Re-mastered from a rescued cassette it was re-released in 2014 by the Australian independent label Metal Postcard, to enthusiastic reviews.

EIGHT

Cambodia's Elvis and the Golden Voice

'From now and for eternity, may we be bonded in every life.'
Sin Sisamouth & Ros Sereysothea, *Thevary My Love*

It seems fitting that a nation with such a deeply-rooted monarchy should have its own rock and roll royalty to revere. Decades after their untimely deaths at the hands of the Khmer Rouge, Sin Sisamouth and Ros Sereysothea remain the undisputed king and queen of Cambodia's music scene. Present day Cambodia has a small but thriving modern music industry, much of it karaoke-fuelled and influenced by Korean pop, though a promising young alternative music scene is also developing, but none of its stars have so far achieved anything like the exalted status that continues to cling to these two time-honoured, national icons.

Sin Sisamouth and Ros Sereysothea made numerous records together

Close personal friends and frequent musical collaborators, the two recorded, and in Sisamouth's case also wrote, thousands of records, mostly as solo artists but also with other popular singers of the time. Their memory, not to mention their retro-cool images taken from the scant, surviving photographic archive, is synonymous with that of Cambodia's Golden Age.

Often referred to as the Elvis of Cambodia, though his silken vocals have far more in common with Nat King Cole, Sin Sisamouth managed what few popular western singers of the day could achieve by making the successful transition from 1950s crooner to best-selling pop star of the 1960s and early 1970s.

Sisamouth was born on 23 August 1932, the year of the rooster (a story goes that at the point of his birth the local cockerels crowed, prophetically, in unison) into a fairly middle class family in Cambodia's Steung Treng province. His father was a prison warden and later joined the military. The young

Sin Sisamouth

Sisamouth developed an early interest in music, learnt to play guitar and performed regularly at school functions. A bright, studious youth, he decided on a medical career but during his studies in Phnom Penh and training at the city's Preah Ketomealea Hospital, he poured equal time and effort into his singing and songwriting. His reward was a regular singing spot on Royal Cambodian Radio while he was still a student.

Sisamouth's sights were obviously set more firmly on music than medicine. His popularity as a singer was growing and in 1951 he was invited to join the palace orchestra, with whom he continued to perform at royal receptions and state functions until the King was deposed in 1970. On graduating, he tied the knot with his cousin Keo Thorng Gnut, an arranged marriage that produced four children but failed to survive the strains imposed by his fame. He later married a dancer from the Royal Ballet with whom he had two more children.

By all accounts Sisamouth was a thoughtful, serious type, a gentle-natured man of few words who preferred to lead a quiet life and was frequently to be found with his nose in a book. Record sleeves consistently portray the singer with a genial expression; clean cut and sharply-dressed.

Sisamouth's early repertoire focused on traditional Khmer songs and folk ballads and his mellifluous tones made him the first and undoubtedly the brightest star of Cambodia's recording industry. In the early 1960s he began recording for the newly-launched Wat Phnom label. Where other singers were contracted to individual record producers, Sisamouth, like Ros Sereysothea, had the professional clout to remain independent, working freely with different labels including Angkor, Independence and Chanchhaya. The name Sin Sisamouth on a record sleeve guaranteed sales, which no doubt explains the many duets he also recorded with fellow singers like Sereysothea, Pan Ron, Huoy Meas, Mao Sareth and Chhun Vanna.

Sisamouth reportedly took immense care over the songs he penned. He wrote the melodies on the mandolin and later added lyrics that were often based on the real-life stories recounted to him by people he knew or met. His singing voice was equally measured, pitch perfect and with clear enunciation.

The cinephile Prince Norodom Sihanouk had inspired a prolific and enthusiastic Cambodian film industry and the singer became its number one soundtrack artist. A rare surviving clip of a Sisamouth performance is in fact taken from the 1966 film, *Apsara*, the story of a classical dancer who is pressured into marrying a military general despite her love for another man, written and directed by the culturally ubiquitous Sihanouk. In it he performs two numbers with singer Sieng Dy at a society wedding party. Other films to be graced by his masterful vocals include *Thevary My Love*, in which he sings two songs including the title track, and *Pov Chouk Sar* starring Dy Saveth, who also duets with Sisamouth on *Snae Chhlong Veha* from the Thai-Khmer collaboration, *Chivit Psong Praeng*. Sisamouth's song *Midday Sun*, recorded with his number one singing partner, Ros Sereysothea, for the Yvon Hem film *Abul Kasem*, scooped the award for Best Film Music at the 1969 Cambodian Film Festival.

Sisamouth's surviving back catalogue is evidence of his versatility as a performer. Early experience working with the palace's classical troupe clearly influenced his technique; he excelled as a balladeer and recorded countless songs in the popular Cuban style. Keen to keep abreast of the country's musical developments he later enlisted the talents of younger musicians to update his repertoire with up tempo rock and roll numbers like *Know How to Dance the Monkey*. He could do no wrong in the eyes of his public.

Following the 1970 coup, Sisamouth was recruited to the military orchestra of the new Khmer Republic, which performed a repertoire of propaganda songs. When Phnom Penh finally fell to the Khmer Rouge in April 1975 he joined the mass eviction of the city.

Accounts of how Sin Sisamouth met his death have, unsurprisingly considering his fame and the uncertainty that surrounds the fate of so many people during the genocide, passed into folklore. The most frequently repeated anecdote suggests that, unable to keep his identity a secret, he was forced to sing for Khmer Rouge guards but was eventually killed when they grew tired of the entertainment.

In 2010 Khmer Radio producer Khut Sokhoeun, with collaborators Pov Sok and Sam Noeun, made a short documentary film about Sisamouth called *Emperor of the Golden Voice*. Their research led them to meet some survivors of a communist work camp in a village in the Koh Thom district of Cambodia's Kandal province who alleged the singer had lived among them. In the evenings, they claimed, he was ordered to sing for the Khmer Rouge elite but as he grew weak from overwork and lack of food he could no longer perform well and was punished, then executed.

'Sisamouth was required to work like other people,' Pov Sok told the *Phnom Penh Post* (10 August 2012) on the film's release. 'Sometimes the militias beat him. People remember seeing scars on his face. Then he was killed and buried under a mango tree. God offered the perfect voice to this man among millions of Cambodian men. His voice was so beautiful to everybody.'

Both Sisamouth's son — one of two who survived the genocide — and grandson would follow him into the music business; sadly they also suffered untimely deaths. Sin Chanchhaya, a talented singer, music teacher and head of the Sin Sisamouth Association set up to protect his father's musical legacy, died at 58 in January 2015 after a fall. His son, singer and sound engineer Sin Sethakol, died of a stroke four years later aged just 37. Sethakol's sister, Setsochhata, has since seized the musical baton and launched her own singing career.

The exquisitely sweet yet singularly powerful vocals that defined Ros Sereysothea's singing style and belied her dainty, five foot frame saw her bestowed a fitting soubriquet by no less a fan than Prince Norodom Sihanouk: the Golden Voice of the Royal Capital.

Born in 1938 in Battambang province, one of five siblings, Sereysothea's upbringing contrasted starkly with that of her friend Sin Sisamouth. The Ros family were poor and life was hard, as it was for many rural Cambodians. Sereysothea loved and excelled at singing from childhood. When her father deserted the family leaving them to support themselves she sang with a music troupe that performed in villages around the province to help make ends meet. Sereysothea's talent caught the ear of the music industry when she entered and won a series of singing contests. Moving to Phnom Penh at the age of 17 she found work — and growing fame — at the national radio station. It was there she met Sin Sisamouth who penned her first record, Blue River, named after a river in her native Battambang. That she would become Sisamouth's most prolific and popular musical partner was inevitable; though the two singers were never romantically involved, their vocals were a match made in heaven.

Ros Sereysothea

Female singers were in no short supply in 1960s Cambodia but Sereysothea was in a class of her own. Her sweetly resonant, crystal-clear soprano readily conveyed profound emotion, even brought her audience to tears, while at other times her delivery was ebullient and playful. Whatever style of song she took on, from lush, string-laden ballads to the dance numbers that resemble a high octane mash-up of psychedelic rock and early Tamla Motown, she put her heart into her singing and her fans gave her theirs in return. It was not Khmer custom to applaud, but audiences would clap spontaneously when Sereysothea began to sing. Though her vocals were charged, she never danced while she performed, unlike other singers of her generation.

Surviving photographs, almost exclusively images from record sleeves, depict a wide cheek-boned beauty with alluring almond eyes and lustrously big hair, sometimes worn in an elegant beehive, sometimes a backcombed bob.

Under the Khmer Republic, Sereysothea exchanged her stylishly-coiffured hair and elegant evening dresses for a new, shorter haircut and army uniform, and her hit songbook for patriotic anthems. Reuters film reel from 18 March 1972 captures her performing with a republican army band before a large crowd gathered at Wat Phnom in the capital.

A surviving piece of propaganda footage shows her on a parachute jump looking waif-like in military fatigues.

Sadly for Sereysothea, the success of her singing career was not mirrored in her romantic relationships; revered by her fans, she was shown less respect by the men in her life. Her first, brief marriage to Sos Mat, a fellow singer who allegedly already had two other wives, lasted a matter of months, turning violent when he grew jealous of the attention she attracted from male admirers. Sereysothea fled back to Battambang to escape the abuse and was only convinced to return to Phnom Penh to continue her career by Sisamouth, who promised her family he would take responsibility for keeping her safe.

Later matches were also ill-fated. A romance with the son of a notable film and record producer led to marriage and the birth of a son but also to another break up. Her relationship with a senior military officer in the republican government that overthrew the King in 1970 produced three more children but ended when he died in combat.

Though the details surrounding Ros Sereysothea's own death are typically undocumented, rumours and hearsay inevitably abound, as indeed they do about her life. Sereysothea died along with her children on the long march from Phnom Penh, go the stories; she was forced into marriage with an abusive senior Khmer Rouge officer. Unable to keep her identity a secret for long in the work camp she was sent to, she had been obliged to perform for Pol Pot's troops before being executed. Others say she had been spotted in an ox cart, driven away by soldiers to her death; even that she was last seen weak and malnourished in a Phnom Penh hospital where she later died. In an award-winning 2006 short film called *Golden Voice*, writer and director Greg Cahill presents a dramatisation of the way Sereysothea's final few months may have unfolded. Fictitious as the screenplay is, the film stands as a poignant tribute to a tragic talent.

Duetting with the snake king's wife

The walls of Dy Saveth's airy Phnom Penh apartment are plastered with photographs that pay eloquent tribute to the *grande dame* of Cambodian cinema's life and distinguished career. The country's most popular and prolific film star, Saveth achieved sudden fame in 1959 when, at 15, the young beauty was crowned the first Miss Cambodia. Film offers followed, Saveth impressed the country's directors as much as its avid cinema-goers and before long she was

Film star Dy Saveth features prominently on the poster for Chivit Psong Praeng.

taking starring roles in opuses like Norodom Sihanouk's *Twilight* ('He had a lot of talent,' she says of the former king, 'he was very good singer. I still think about him'); *Pous Keng Kang,* a.k.a. *The Snake King's Wife* and *Chivit Psong Praeng,* in which she shared a duet with Sin Sisamouth.

Still poised, elegant and remarkably youthful in her 70s, Saveth remembers how awed she first felt at the thought of singing with the 'Emperor of Song'. While she liked to sing, her voice, she believed, did not have the quality of Cambodian performers of the day. 'Sin Sisamouth came to my house to teach me,' she recounts. 'He was a very nice guy, very calm, he didn't talk too much. He told me not to be shy, not to be afraid. He explained a lot to me.'

Saveth remembers the nightclubs where the newly popular a-go-go dancing was all the rage but says she preferred to go home after working rather than socialise: 'Everybody who loved dancing went to the Nightclub D'Etat, the musicians and singers were very good'.

As fate would have it, Saveth was in Thailand when Pol Pot's army seized Phnom Penh. Unable to return home, she moved to France where she spent the best part of two decades and put her acting career behind her. But Saveth's fans would not let her retire for good. When she finally returned to Cambodia in 1993, she was encouraged to resume her film career and now also teaches performance arts at the Royal University of Phnom Penh to a coterie of devoted students.

NINE
Don't Miss Me

'I picture you like a star, shining out of arm's reach.'
Ros Sereysothea, A-go-go

In the notional Cambodian Rock and Roll Hall of Fame, one artist in particular occupies an exalted position alongside Sin Sisamouth and Ros Sereysothea. Pan Ron, also known as Pen Ran, our sassy songstress from Chapter One, is the certified crown princess of Golden Age music with a prodigious repertoire of songs to her name and a groovy image that made her a particular favourite with the *Sangkum's* young set. Her lyrics were often teasingly playful, her performances more animated, her skirts perhaps a touch shorter, her hairdo a little perkier than those of her peers. Here was a spirited, modern, young female who, in a society where a woman's role was mired in traditional expectations, dared if not exactly to push the envelope, then at least to exert a little gentle pressure on it.

Pop princess Pan Ron

A duet with Sin Sisamouth in 1966 proved a major boost for Ron's already buoyant singing career and led to a string of hits that included more collaborations with Sisamouth and with other popular artists like Ros Sereysothea, Meas Samoun and Eng Nary. Her canon ranged from tear jerker ballads to the frenetic twist 'n' shout of one of her most popularly remembered hits, *I'm Unsatisfied*, still guaranteed to get an audience on its feet before the opening bars have played out.

Despite her widespread fame little is documented or remembered of Pan Ron's life beyond her musical legacy. It's believed she was brought up by nuns after being abandoned as a baby at a Catholic orphanage in Battambang. Like many of the era's young singing stars her career began when she won a singing contest and began touring with the orchestral troupe that accompanied the King on his official trips to the Cambodian provinces. Actress Dy Saveth remembers a lively, outgoing young woman who 'loved talking and laughing; when she sang the young boys and girls loved to sing with her.'

Details of Ron's death are equally unclear though it's certain she failed to survive the Pol Pot regime. Alleged eyewitness sightings suggest she perished at Wat Troap Kor in the Bati district of Takeo province, executed by communist soldiers along with a group of thirty or so men, women and children, including her own four offspring. The Troap Kor pagoda has been declared a genocide memorial site following the discovery there of over seventy mass graves, holding the remains of 30 – 40,000 victims of the Khmer Rouge. Whether or not Pan Ron was among them, the death toll at this formerly peaceful place of Buddhist worship was among the heaviest of the genocide years.

As we've seen, popular music in Cambodia was in the business of rocking the people not the establishment. If there was a rebel in its midst, that man was Yol Aularong. Aularong's image, if not exactly subversive by western standards was certainly less conformist than those of his contemporaries. The young singer, guitarist and songwriter is remembered as a wayward personality who was disinclined to bow to authority. His surviving recordings from the early 1970s epitomise Khmer garage rock: raw, rough around the edges and a little crazy. Images of Aularong are hard to come by but rare footage of him performing at an outdoor event shows a young man with a mop of unruly hair, guitar slung across his shoulder.

His songs, meanwhile, tended to eschew the overtly romantic in favour of more observational lyrics, often cheekily satirical. From *Broken Hearted Bachelor*, a storming subversion of Van Morrison's *Gloria* and the cocky, quirky humour of *Riding a Cyclo*; to *Whiskey Whiskey*, a bluesy, drunken paean to sra, Cambodia's notorious rice-based hooch and the belligerent drive of *Black Coffee*, his punk attitude and willingness to mock convention set him aside from his contemporaries.

Bad boy Yol Aularong

Drakkar's Touch Seang Tana, who gave him his first recording opportunity on a compilation cassette he produced in the early 1970s — the song in question, *Navany*, also known as *Number One*, propelled him to fame — says Aularong was born into a large, affluent family. His father worked for the French Embassy and split his time between France and Phnom Penh but ill health had forced him to retire early, leaving the family in impoverished circumstances. Tana and Aularong played together in a rhythm and blues band that performed at the US embassy before the latter secured a regular spot at a jazz club owned by an uncle who was himself a talented musician.

While Aularong's exact fate is unknown — like so many of his peers he simply disappeared — commentators have

Joker in the pack Meas Samoun

suggested his headstrong manner would have led to an early clash with Khmer Rouge authorities.

If Sin Sisamouth and Ros Sereysothea are the king and queen of Golden Age music and Yol Aularong the smart-ass knave, then the joker in the pack is certainly Meas Samoun. With his Charlie Chaplin moustache (the comedian visited Cambodia in 1936 and made a big impact on the people; to this day Khmer comedians are inclined to sport a Chaplinesque growth on their upper lips) and humorous, gruff voice, his image was as comedic as his songs. The comic was frequently and popularly paired with female singer So Savouen. Whereas Samoun is presumed to have died in a Khmer Rouge labour camp, Savouen was more fortunate. She and her husband escaped the regime with a timely move to Thailand, later travelling to France where she still lives.

Singing sisters Sieng Vanthy and Sieng Dy, aunts of Yol Aularong, were also among the few famous singers who survived the regime. The pair were born into a family of entertainers from Prey Veng province; their father was a comedian and their mother an actress in a traditional theatre troupe. Both found initial success as members of the singing troupe belonging to the state-owned brewery, Société Khmère de Distillerie. Vanthy died aged 61 in December 2009 in a Phnom Penh hospital, having given up in the mid-1990s the singing career she continued post-Khmer Rouge. Dy married into Cambodian royalty when she tied the knot with Prince Sisowath Chariya but was widowed in 2017. She died in August 2019 in a US hospital following a serious fall.

Two Norodom Sihanouk-directed films, *Apsara* and *La Joie de Vivre*, copies of which have happily been preserved in the royal archives, afford not only a seductive glimpse into the spirit of the era but also an extremely rare opportunity to see some of its musical stars in action. In *Apsara*, Sieng Dy duets with Sin Sisamouth on two numbers during a party scene, while in *La Joie de Vivre*, where she also takes a cameo acting role, she performs *Rom A-go-go*, a song recorded by Pan Ron. The latter film also features an appearance by So Savouen — and some extremely funky dancing!

La Joie de Vivre is also notable for a brief but unforgettable (and uncredited) cameo by a gravel-voiced singer identified as Liv Tek (also referred to as Liev Tuk and credited on the Cambodia Rocks compilation albums as Lelu Thaert). His energetic, arm-flailing performance in the film along with a record, *Soul Dancing* — actually a version of Booker T's instrumental hit, *Hip Hug Her* with Khmer lyrics added — a couple of ballads, some screaming on Yol Aularong's

Girl-next-door Houy Meas

raucous *Rather Die Under a Woman's Sword* and one very grainy photo appear to be all that's left to remember him by.

A natural beauty, softly spoken with a modest manner and captivating singing voice, Houy Meas exemplified the Cambodian female ideal. Like her friends and peers Pan Ron and Ros Sereysothea, Meas struck out from her native Battambang to make her name as a singer in Phnom Penh, where her sweetly agreeable voice and girl-next-door persona meant she was also in demand as a presenter and sometime actress on Royal Cambodian Radio. Musically, she specialised in tender, often heart-wrenching ballads. Despite her fame, it's believed that Meas was able to hide her identity from Khmer Rouge officials until 1977, when she was outed and killed.

An earlier wave of female performers inspired the careers of the stars who rose to success in the 1960s. Mao Sareth, Chhun Vanna and Chhoun Malay, sublime singers in their own right, achieved fame in the late 1950s before rock music made its mark in the Kingdom and enjoyed successful recording careers throughout the 1960s. Both Malay and Vanna survived the genocide, settling in the US before their deaths in 2012 and 2019 respectively.

Of the era's galaxy of singing stars, Pov Vannary's career was probably the shortest-lived. Vannary made a string of

Chhun Vanna and Chhuon Malay paved the way for later singing stars

Images courtesy CVMA

recordings in the early 1970s when dark clouds of change were descending on the previously swinging capital.

Cambodia's Golden Age was over, the monarchy overthrown leaving Norodom Sihanouk exiled in Beijing and Lon Nol's US-backed Khmer Republic in power. The freedoms, artistic and otherwise, that had previously flourished were gradually eroded not only by the authoritarianism of the new political regime but also by the encroaching civil war. As the 1970s progressed, Pol Pot's communist forces stepped up their gradual takeover of the provinces, advancing further and further on the final stronghold of Phnom Penh. Khmer Republic troops skirmished with enemy soldiers ever nearer its outlying suburbs and the sounds of gunfire and mortar attacks began to permeate the soundtrack of daily life. Curfews were imposed, night clubs ceased to operate and musicians were ultimately left with little option but to perform propagandist songs for the government. Sporadic grenade attacks forced ever the city's beloved cinemas to eventually close their doors. In the early years of the decade, however, the average citizen knew little of what loomed on their doorstep; life went on and music was still a part of it.

Vannary is remembered for 'Americanising' Khmer pop music, and certainly the young singer took foreign influences further than her predecessors. The late 1960s had seen the rise of singer songwriters in the US in particular. Vannary chose a more westernised vocal delivery over the comparatively formal technique, with its precise intonation and high register, traditionally associated with female Khmer singers and still favoured by her contemporaries. She also broke with tradition by accompanying herself on guitar, the first female Cambodian singer to do so, adopting a performance style more reminiscent of Joni Mitchell and Carole King than the likes of Pan Ron and Ros Sereysothea. One of her best remembered recordings is King's *You've Got A Friend*, sung like many of her hits in a mix of English and Khmer. She gave the same treatment, shifting between languages, to haunting covers of Harry Nilsson's *Without You* and Carpenters' hits *Yesterday Once More* and (the Leon Russell/Delaney and Bonnie composition) *Superstar*.

Guitar girl Pov Vannary

Image courtesy CVMA

Would more women have followed her lead; picked up guitars, found success as musicians and songwriters and invaded that hitherto male-dominated side of the music industry had the country's culture not been effectively annihilated? Pov Vannary had little time to influence any such evolution. She failed to survive the genocide and the facts surrounding her death remain as much a mystery as those of so many of her fellows.

Battambang blues

An arresting mural adorns a wall of the Madison Corner bar in downtown Battambang. Two larger-than-life faces observe patrons and passers-by with a certain amused benevolence. The likeness to local hero Ros Sereysothea and her musical consort Sin Sisamouth may be slightly questionable but not the sincerity of the tribute to the two golden greats; and to Battambang's singular contribution to Cambodia's rock and roll history.

Was it something in the water of the Sangke River, also known as the *Steung Khieu*, or Blue River, and immortalised in Ros Sereysothea's hit record of the same name that nourished a generation of musical talent? The waterway snakes lazily through Cambodia's second city and across Battambang province, where not only Sereysothea but also Pan Ron, Houy Meas, fellow singers Mao Sareth (another victim of the Khmer Rouge) and Im Song Soem (who died of lung cancer in 1973) were all born in the 1930s.

Prolific songwriters Vo Hoy and Kong Bunchhoeun were also native Battambangers. Bunchhoeun, who succumbed to cancer in Norway in 2016 was equally a notable poet, painter, film maker and a controversial novelist who frequently praised the beauty of his native province, and by association, its women, in song and verse. He and his wife came close to being executed by the Khmer Rouge but were reportedly saved by officers who had read his books and made the case for his work as being supportive of the class struggle.

Of a number of musical homages to Battambang, two sung by Sin Sisamouth who also made his home there at one point, are probably the best remembered: *Flower of the River Sangke* and *Flower of Battambang*.

Cambodia's second city, in the country's north east some 100 kilometres from the Thai border, was developed as an urban centre by the French in the 1930s. Post-Independence, as a key administrative hub for Prince Norodom Sihanouk's government it was treated to a round of expansion and modernisation that updated its genteel colonial character with architecture of the starkly modernist New Khmer style. Back in the day Battambang had a flourishing social scene and the Blue River Lounge on the waterfront served as its hub, hosting performances by many of the country's best known artists including Sereysothea herself. When Khmer Rouge troops eventually captured the city its inhabitants, like the citizens of Phnom Penh, were dispatched to the countryside and the same, grim fate.

TEN

The Collectors

'Some people are dedicated...'.
Yol Aularong, *Number One*

Attempts to document Cambodian life before Pol Pot's short but devastating command are routinely derailed by the shocking fact that his regime's fixation on a return to Year Zero came close to erasing the country's modern history. The wrecking ball that was Khmer Rouge policy targeted all aspects of contemporary, 'bourgeois' life, particularly that influenced by the decadent West. Film, television and newsreel footage, photographs, records and master tapes together with the studios where they were produced were destroyed. Popular culture was obliterated, civic society completely dismantled and public buildings and their contents abandoned. Most of what material remains have survived were saved by those who managed to flee the country in advance of the fall of Phnom Penh.

Not only were public artefacts and private possessions alike destroyed en masse, but the loss of so many lives — up to a possible third of the country's population — meant that valuable elements of oral history were also stolen. Whole families were wiped out; the memories of survivors, meanwhile, are frequently impaired by age and trauma.

Under the Khmer Rouge, personal possessions were strictly prohibited. To hold on to them meant risking punishment or even death; in the work camps even the smallest transgressions led to brutal penalties. Rather than hand them over to the authorities, in desperation many people chose to bury valued possessions like precious photographs and other keepsakes without knowing if they or their relatives would ever return to unearth them. Vinyl records were among the treasures interred.

Oum Rotanak Oudom, known to all as Oro, has devoted much of his spare time and most of his spare cash to his longtime passion: collecting, archiving and sharing online original Cambodian records. The personable Phnom Penh-born musicologist and sometime DJ formalised his preoccupation with Golden Age music in 2011 when, together with Americans Maya Jade and Nate Hun, he established the Cambodian Vintage Music Archive (CVMA), a non-profit project committed to preserving and promoting the legacy of the music and of the artists who made it at least a decade before he was born.

Every picture tells a story

'The music truly represents the heart of Cambodian contemporary culture in the 60s and 70s,' explains Oro. 'I started to listen to the old songs when I was a child, maybe around six or seven years old. I fell in love with the music even though I knew nothing about it.'

Today the same songs by the same artists filter into the consciousness of a new generation of youngsters. But the versions they hear on TV, radio or played by their parents, like those that so entranced the young Oro, may well sound different to the originals. In the late 1980s and early 1990s, as life in Cambodia edged back to some kind of normality, the music banned by the Khmer Rouge began to re-emerge in the form of compilation tapes and CDs generated from what surviving records came to light. But the source material was often damaged and the poor sound quality that resulted was degraded further through repeated copying. The producers of these compilations were not precious about their treatment of the songs, as Oro explains:

'Most of the old records were remixed, adding synthetic instrument fills. I bought many of those remixed CDs and was disappointed to hear my favourite artists sing at distorted speeds over the cacophony of garish synthesiser effects. They butchered these beautiful songs and it inspired me to find the originals and ensure they are properly archived.'

The proliferation of these remixes can make it hard to know if what you're hearing is the real thing but Oro reckons that the online sharing of original recordings by CVMA and a

Images courtesy CVMA

number of other, mainly American fans is educating listeners to distinguish between the authentic sounds and the doctored versions.

Oro met Maya Jade in his then home city of Phnom Penh at a New Year party held by French Cambodian film maker Davy Chou, grandson of the noted Golden Age movie producer, Van Chann. The pair bonded over their mutual love of Cambodian music and decided to pool their efforts and financial resources to bring as many as possible of the old songs to new life in a restored digital format. Oro got to know fellow music historian Nate through the latter's YouTube channel showcasing Khmer music and film. They finally met when both were invited to speak at a Cambodian pop culture event in Phnom Penh.

Two elements, the founders agreed, would be central to CVMA's approach: the use of the best high fidelity equipment they could afford so as to preserve the integrity of the original recordings and restore the sound quality; and a commitment to ensuring the surviving artists and the families of the many who died received the royalties due.

Oro's personal collection numbers over a hundred records. Nate, he says, has amassed a similar volume and CVMA has digitised hundreds more records owned and loaned by private collectors. 'We have some people donating records to our project and some donating the digital files,' he explains. 'It's very important that the donor or fan are people who care about the music and want to share in the proper legal manner.'

Oro explains how he came by the largest single collection of vintage records acquired by the archive, some 25 pieces of rare vinyl. Vintage Cambodian vinyl is rarely, if ever these days, to be found in the country's shops and markets, and collectors' fairs are unheard of; the key to vinyl sleuthing is keeping an ear to the ground, from where a good number of surviving records have been quite literally unearthed.

Oro had heard of a collector reportedly living in the rural village of Koh Kae in Kampong Cham province some sixty miles outside the capital. Beyond that he had nothing to go on but set off on his mission nonetheless, aided and abetted

Images courtesy CVMA

by a young volunteer worker he had met by chance and whose parents lived in the village in question.

'His name was Taki Hero,' Oro recalls, 'and he drove me a long way on his old bike along a very difficult road with rain and dirt everywhere. When we arrived I started searching for the collector, just asking from house to house or of any people around whether or not they have seen this vinyl and if they know who is the collector.'

In a local pagoda the pair met a monk who told them he was aware that a pile of records had been left there for safekeeping directly before the communist forces took over. They had been stacked, he said, or the floor of the building, where the Khmer Rouge had discovered them and ordered their destruction. All very interesting, but it left Oro no nearer his goal.

'I was tired from riding on the dusty roads from village to village, feeling hopeless,' he says. 'I went back to Hero's house and spent the night in his parents' little hut.'

The next morning brought a last-ditch attempt to find the collector before Oro had to return home to Phnom Penh, and with it a lucky break. The aptly-named Hero drove him to the house of a retired teacher called Nong Neang. The 75-year old, by then in poor health, had been a painter and musician during the 1960s.

'He showed me his paintings and played his mandolin for me,' recounts Oro, 'and we talked about vinyl. Then he told me that during the 1980s he was a rice farmer. He went to

Phnom Penh to sell rice and exchanged some of his crop for records but did not remember where he had put them. He had stacks of boxes in his store rooms covered in dust. We went from room to room searching for the box he had hidden his records in, it took some time for us to find them and when we did I was really excited.'

Oro says he had hoped only for permission to digitise the elderly man's records for the archive but, 'after we had talked passionately about how wonderful the music was, he said "I am old and I know you are the best person to take care of them for me. I will give all my records to you." '

Overwhelmed, Oro thanked his benefactor profusely, promising to take good care of the records for him.

'After I got back to Phnom Penh I digitised his records, burned them onto a flash drive and sent them to him. He told me that he hadn't listened to the records since the 1980s.'

For Oro and his CVMA colleagues there is an unfortunate downside to the growing interest in Cambodia's vintage music: the rising cost of original records driven by an increase in the number of collectors worldwide.

'They were not very expensive at the beginning, around twenty to fifty US dollars depending on the condition. However, people began to see the rarity value, which unfortunately means prices have been getting more expensive. It's a small market targeting both local and foreign buyers. Some of the sellers are not aware that records were reprinted in the late 80s and 90s. The records are sold on eBay and other commercial websites regardless of whether they are originals or reissues, in bad or good condition.

'As matter of fact, I cannot afford to buy a record that is sold on eBay now. For instance, one 7-inch record may be around $200 to $500 while a 12-inch is $500 to $1,500.'

'Youtube is really the only place you can find original [Khmer] music to hear and enjoy without actually having the record in front of you.'

So observes US-born Samrach Touch, for whom the old songs have a particular resonance by providing a valuable link to the culture of his parents and grandparents. Sam was inspired by the Cambodian Vintage Music Archive to share his own collection of vintage vinyl with the community of fans who go online to soak up the sounds of 1960s and 70s Cambodia, many of whom, like Sam himself, are young people of Khmer descent living in the Cambodian diaspora.

Sam's father emigrated to the US from Cambodia with his own parents to escape the Pol Pot regime and met his American wife in the States. 'I've always been exposed to the music of Cambodia,' Sam recalls, 'my grandmother and grandfather would listen to it every day and night, but it wasn't until I was about ten or eleven that I started to really take a liking to it.'

His cache of highly collectable vinyl numbers about fifty pieces, most of it sourced from France and Cambodia. Finding decent quality records and at an affordable price, he emphasises, takes some effort:

'Buying from Cambodia you are more or less going to see records that are dirty, cracked or chipped and most people won't sell as they have a very strong attachment to them. Every now and then one will pop up on eBay from France but most are very expensive. In America they're almost non-existent, I've only found two and that was by sheer luck.

'Music is a huge part of our culture and heritage. Cambodian music is very much from the heart and soul, written of the singers' own experiences and feelings. In a way this music is a part of who they are. I feel that as one of the first generation of Cambodian American people I have a certain duty to carry on and preserve this music and history for future generations to enjoy.'

Art on their sleeves

For lovers of original vinyl, even those without a personal or emotional connection to the country, vintage Cambodian records have an appeal that extends beyond their rarity value. The compelling history behind the collectors' pieces is one factor, another is the iconic cover art. Sometimes kitsch, often gloriously chromatic and irresistibly evocative of the era, the images that graced the 7-inch sleeves included stylised film stills, crazy photographic montages and original artworks by artists like Nhek Dim.

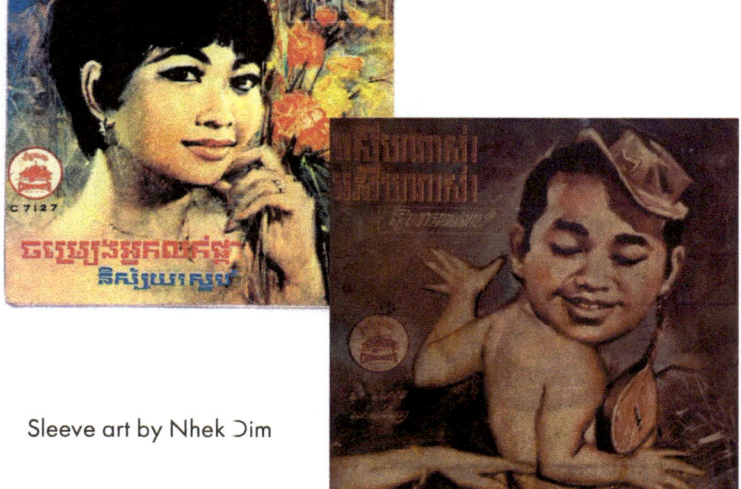

Sleeve art by Nhek Dim

Dim was yet another talent lost to the Khmer Rouge. A graduate of the Cambodian School of Arts and favourite of Norodom Sihanouk, he studied cartoon film making in the US and was also known as a novelist and composer. His work for record labels included many portraits of the major artists, from delicate watercolour renderings of singers like Ros Sereysothea to a clever caricature of a baby Sin Sisamouth complete with trilby and mandolin that illustrates the singer's 1973 hit *I'm Ticklish*.

ELEVEN

City of Tears

'I sing of hopelessness, I hear thunder but there is no rain. The earth is dry and barren, my heart is broken. There is no hope of your return.'

Sieng Dy, *Song of Hopelessness.*

When the residue of Phnom Penh's former inhabitants trickled slowly back to the capital in early 1979, numbed and bereft, they discovered a city that was equally stricken. Forcibly and suddenly abandoned by the families who had called them home, the city's former dwellings lay derelict and desolate, one-time possessions piled in broken heaps. Many public buildings were reduced to rubble and vegetation was beginning to reclaim the streets. The Pearl of Asia was now a city of tears, its life snuffed out like that of so many of its former inhabitants. Returnees settled where they could and waited for news of their families and friends. News that for many would never arrive.

Not only had there been a catastrophic loss of life — among those dead or disappeared the teachers, doctors, lawyers, civil servants and bankers; the bastions of civil society — but the country's economy, its infrastructure and institutions had been decimated. Survivors had no idea what the future held for them. It would be a long and hard path back to any kind of normality for a nation so comprehensively brutalised.

Singer Sieng Vanthy was among the first to make the painful return to Phnom Penh. Vanthy, who died in 2009, told film maker John Pirozzi in his documentary *Don't Think I've Forgotten:*

'They were looking for artists and recognised me as Sieng Vanthy. I sang on the radio for everyone. People were scared to come back to Phnom Penh. When the surviving artists heard my voice they felt safe to return. Those who didn't return were considered dead.'

Vanthy herself, separated from her family and forced into hard labour, had managed to survive by hiding her true identity and passing herself off as a fruit seller. Life in the rural work camps had been unimaginably tough for all. In line with the regime's hardline Maoist principles the family unit was outlawed, husbands and wives were separated and children torn from their parents to work the fields like adults. The so-called 'new people', the forced emigrants of Phnom Penh and other cities had the worst of it, targeted by Khmer Rouge guards and treated with suspicion and mistrust by the rural locals they were now toiling alongside. The labour involved was relentless, food was scarce and conditions bleak and inhuman. Death hovered in plain sight at all times, from overwork, malnutrition and routine executions. At Cambodia's 'killing fields' as they have come to be known, victims were slain en masse — often bludgeoned to death as munitions were deemed a needless expense — frequently for arbitrary and contrived offences and their bodies dumped unceremoniously in ditches and pits. No records were kept of these casualties, a generation lost to four barbaric years in history.

The Khmer Rouge was overthrown in early 1979 by Vietnamese troops who finally captured Phnom Penh on 7 January, forcing Pol Pot and what remained of his forces to retreat into the Cambodian jungle. It would take nearly two more decades, a United Nations intervention and some complex political manoeuvring before the country was finally returned to peace and stability. Pol Pot himself died on 15 April 1998 while held under house arrest by members of his own party.

The Documentation Centre of Cambodia (DC Cam) was established in 1995, one of its key missions to chronicle for posterity the stories of survivors. The disturbing testimonies the organisation has painstakingly notarised provide a picture of the atrocities inflicted on an innocent population, the ramifications of which are still evident today. A report from 2005 on the Victims of Trauma project, carried out by DC Cam and the Transcultural Psychosocial Organization of Cambodia to assess and address the psychological effects of the genocide on survivors, stated that 28.4% of

Cambodians had been found to suffer from post-traumatic stress disorder, 11.5% from mood disorders, and 40% from anxiety disorders.

Youk Chhang is Executive Director of DC Cam and the 2018 recipient of a Ramon Magsaysay Award, Asia's version of a Nobel Prize. In an interview with the *Al Jazeera America* news channel (9 April 2014) Chhang, himself the survivor of a Khmer Rouge work camp, described music as 'a way of healing and caring for Khmer society.'

'Without healing, and dealing with the past,' he adds, 'it would be difficult for Cambodians to move forward. I want to move on with my life along with all other genocide survivors. Music is magical, and can bring both heritage and contemporary feelings to all; to heal. Music can also help restore what we have lost.'

So many of the artists were dead but the songs they sang remained in the hearts and minds of the living; bittersweet links to a former life.

Survivors' Songs

As Khmer Rouge control weakened in the face of the Vietnamese offensive, many survivors of the labour camps made their often perilous way to refugee camps on the Thai border.

The Vietnamese army may have forced an end to Khmer Rouge rule but to many Cambodians they were still an occupying force in a country that had only relatively recently freed itself from foreign intervention. Musician and prolific composer of songs for the likes of Ros Sereysothea and Sin Sisamouth, Oum Dara found refuge at a camp in the Banteay Ampil district of Oddar Meanchey province where he wrote a series of new songs that aimed to fuel the spirit of resistance against the Vietnamese. Dara performed these songs, as powerful as they are poignant, with what became known as the Banteay Ampil Band, using handmade and cobbled together instruments.

Eventually released in 1983, *Cambodian Liberation Songs* was the first recording of Cambodian music to be made after the genocide and a chance for surviving Khmer musicians and singers to to vent their anger and sadness in songs that ran the gamut from traditionally-inspired ballads to full-on rock numbers with titles like *Please Avenge my Blood, Darling*.

Born in 1940 in Kampong Cham, Dara had learned to play the violin as a young teenager. In the early 1960s, like many of his fellow musicians, he left his provincial home for the capital to join the growing ranks of professional musicians working at the national radio station. Before long he was also writing music and song lyrics for its star performers, earning fame and a degree of fortune in the process.

All of that changed in April 1975 when the Khmer Rouge captured Phnom Penh. Forced out of the capital to rural Kandal province, Dara was recognised by a Khmer Rouge official and recruited to play violin in a troupe that performed propagandist songs. Not a role he was happy with but one that saved his life. After the war Dara found work as a music teacher and composer with the Ministry of Information. Today, partially disabled following a motorbike accident he lives a simple life with his second wife in Phnom Penh.

១២

TWELVE

A Journey Through Time and Space

'In the light of a new dawn it's our time.'
Astronomy Class & Kak Channthy, Cook Angry Bird in Ginger

'There's a whole lot of wats, and a whole lot of whys.' Phnom Penh-based ex-pat singer songwriter and musician Scott Bywater artfully sums up the allure of the Kingdom of Wonder and of a culture that frequently baffles as it simultaneously beguiles the many foreigners drawn to its shores. Cambodia's vintage rock and rollers had borrowed freely and creatively from the west; decades on, western musicians seduced as much by the sounds of the country as its sights are returning the compliment, working creatively with their Khmer peers and in the process helping to introduce the music to a new, more global fan base.

Bywater, from Hobart, Tasmania, was a formative member of the Cambodian Space Project, a hybrid of Khmer and *barang* (or westerner) musicians, who spent the best part of a decade reviving and re-imagining Cambodian psychedelic rock and roll for local and international audiences alike.

The band's founder, fellow Hobart native Julien Poulson, arrived in Cambodia with the intention of developing a music-focused volunteer programme he'd been working on in East Timor. Lured by his love of psychedelic rock — and of a Khmer beauty called Kak Channthy — he embarked instead on an unexpected space odyssey.

Poulson had been researching a documentary that would explore Cambodia via the eclectic medium of its music.

'We were looking at performers from all walks of life,' he says, 'and that included the bar girls whom I'd noticed doing this *ayay* thing [a form of comedy sparring between two singers, somewhere between a song and a rap and usually accompanied by traditional instruments] – very cool.' One of the girls he recorded suggested Julien meet a friend she worked with who had a great singing voice. He duly turned up at a bar named Black Cat and ran straight into the woman who would become his wife and musical partner, though he admits, 'I don't know to this day if she was the person I was supposed to meet.'

It was Kak Channthy's second week in the job and she had next to no English. For want of a better overture he handed the young woman his headphones, to listen to a 1960s

Khmer music compilation he had with him, and was blown away when she broke into the grooviest of go-go dances. 'She lit up,' Poulson remembers, 'I thought "this is someone who should be on a stage." '

Fortunately Channthy's voice proved as captivating as her dance moves. The couple's relationship developed in sync with the music they began working on together and Cambodian Space Project's first official outing was in 2009 at a Phnom Penh back street bar called Alley Cat, where they played the few songs they knew, all Khmer pop classics, several times over.

The band's repertoire grew along with its line up, a fluctuating assemblage of creative, multi-national members and collaborators, who took Khmer rock and roll and then took liberties, much as Cambodian music had with the western sounds that inspired it, to produce a revved-up barrage of psychedelic sound overlaid with Channthy's supercharged, alto vocals.

Cambodian Space Project produced five internationally-acclaimed albums. A 2015 documentary about the band, *Not Easy Rock and Roll* has aired on Australian and UK TV. Though Julien and Channthy divorced in 2017 they remained close friends as well as co-pilots.

Tragically, Channthy's personal story is of another gifted Khmer chanteuse cut down in her prime. On the early morning of 20 March 2018, Cambodia's Golden Age music lost its single most compelling contemporary ambassador in

Lost in Space: Srey Thy in Melbourne, 2014

a Phnom Penh traffic accident. She was 38, about the age her hero Pan Ron would also have lost her life.

The singer known to many as Srey Thy was a charismatic front-woman. Her interpretations of vintage classics were as fresh as they were faithful to the spirit of the original artists and her exuberant performances were laced with disarmingly open anecdotes about her life. In a 2014 interview for the Grantourismo website the single mum brought up in poverty among the rice fields of rural Prey Veng province in the immediate aftermath of the Pol Pot regime talked about her family and childhood:

'When I was born Cambodia was freer but it was still war ... we did not have what you would imagine as a house and a home life. My father was moving around with the army. We went to the conflict zones. My two siblings died from starvation. This was just the situation, almost normal at the time.

'I remember my mum singing to me from an early age. I remember and know many of her favourite songs. From a young age I went to work alone. I just had the old songs in my head, thanks to my mum and what I would learn from the radio.'

In 2001 a bunch of Californian musicians began their own creative experiment with Khmer rock. Inspired by the psychedelic sounds that had captured his imagination while travelling Cambodia in the late 1990s, LA-based keyboard player Ethan Holtzman joined up with his guitarist brother Zac to form the band Dengue Fever.

'The music was familiar but different,' he recalls, 'it reminded me of bands I grew up listening to like The Ventures, Blondie or The Doors, only the vocals were on another level. The Cambodian female lead vocal added something unique and powerful.'

With bass player Senon Williams, saxophonist David Ralicke, and drummer, Paul Smith on board, all the band needed was a singer.

'At the beginning we didn't know that there was a large Cambodian population in Long Beach, California, about a thirty minute drive from our neighbourhood,' Ethan admits, 'Once we realised it was possible to find [a Cambodian singer] we were dead set on it.'

That singer turned out to be Chhom Nimol. Brought up in a Thai refugee camp during the Khmer Rouge regime, Nimol had already had some success as a singer in her native Cambodia before emigrating to the US and her vocals, like those of her predecessors from the 1960s, were hauntingly charismatic.

It's one thing to embrace the music of a foreign culture, quite another to take that music back to its country of origin and perform it before a local audience. Ethan says that Khmer music fans have always been 'really warm and receptive' to the band but concedes that Dengue Fever's first visit to Cambodia, captured on the album and accompanying DVD *Sleepwalking Through the Mekong*, was a little nerve-racking:

'We were the first westerners to tour Cambodia playing this style of music. We weren't sure how the locals would respond. Ultimately, it brought everybody together. There was an excitement that spilled outside of the club and into the streets. Everyone was dancing. The Cambodians and westerners, who at the time hung out for the most part separate from each other, just intermingled and all inhibitions were gone.'

Dengue Fever have garnered global praise for their characteristic fusion of Cambodian rock and exhilarating live performances. While their early albums favoured covers of Khmer classics, later recordings have focused on original material written in English and translated to Khmer and their songs have graced film and TV soundtracks including the 2002 film *City of Ghosts*.

The Matt Dillon-directed movie portrays the 'wild east' city that was Phnom Penh at the turn of the 1990s in evocative 35mm. John Pirozzi, a cinematographer working on the film, was so captivated by his experience of the country and in particular the music showcased in its soundtrack — which also features songs by Ros Sereysothea, Sin Sisamouth, Pan Ron and Meas Samouen — that he set about researching the artists and their history. The result is the 2014 documentary, *Don't Think I've Forgotten*, a masterful exploration of and tribute to the era, its singular charm and ultimate tragedy.

Pirozzi says the documentary was ten years in the making. 'The problem was there was no primary research to go to, no-one had written about it at that point,' he told the *Phnom Penh Post* (10 January 2014) on the film's premier in the capital, 'so I was starting out with just a few names: Sin Sisamouth, Ros Sereysothea. I really wanted the film to give a sense that there was this comprehensive music scene. It wasn't just a few random singers. It was very rich with many different types of music.'

The film, which includes interviews with surviving players from the period, has attracted significant acclaim. *Rolling Stone* magazine (28 April 2015) calls it 'captivating' and says it 'deftly encapsulates this 1960s history and the importance and popularity of music to the country ... that the documentary exists at all is a triumph, given that officials destroyed many of the era's recordings.'

Rock and roll, notorious as it is for hedonism and excess, has racked up its share of casualties on a global scale, many of legendary status. Jimi Hendrix, Jim Morrison, Kurt Cobain, Amy Winehouse and their peer members of the so-called 27 club, a post-mortem roll-call of famous musicians who died at the same, premature age, exemplify the ethos of 'live fast, die young'.

Cambodia's lost generation of singers, musicians and songwriters were victims not of the fallout of a reckless lifestyle or of the pressures imposed by fame but of a brutal regime that sought to eliminate its perceived enemies and all but destroyed its own country in the process.

Lives may be lost on a monstrous scale, cities wrecked, society as a whole dismantled, but the soul of a nation is not so easily extinguished. Cambodia's illustrious, idiosyncratic music lives on; in the hearts of Khmer people, in the enterprise of evangelical fans and through a new generation of accomplished musicians both Khmer and foreign; while its tragic backstory confers upon the revered artists who made it, their own, singular brand of immortality.

Image courtesy CVMA

Acknowledgements

My immense gratitude to Mol Kagnol, Touch Seang Tana and everyone who agreed to be interviewed for this book. I'm indebted to Oro in particular for his additional help and for allowing me access to Cambodian Vintage Music Archive's remarkable catalogue of record sleeve images. Thanks also to Steve Millward for invaluable advice and support, to Abbie Wraige for being my PO Box and much more, to An Sopheaktra at Bophana and to Nate Hun for some of the lyric translations.

Last, but never least in my hierarchy of appreciation, is Graham Haythorpe — where would I be without his wisdom and patience?

Resources

The Cambodian Vintage Music Archive
Bophana Audiovisual Resource Centre
Cambodian Living Arts
The Documentation Centre of Cambodia (DC-Cam)
Cultures Of Independence: An introduction to Cambodian Arts and Culture in the 1960s and 1970's (Reyum Publishing 2001)
When The War Was Over – Elizabeth Becker (Public Affairs 1998)
The Pol Pot Regime – Ben Kiernan (Silkworm Books 1996)
Cambodia Daily
Khmer Times
Phnom Penh Post
Don't Think I've Forgotten (Dir. John Pirozzi, 2014)
www.dynamickhmerblogspot.com
www.khmermusic.thecoleranch.com

For exclusive discounts on Matador titles,
sign up to our occasional newsletter at
troubador.co.uk/bookshop